UNDER SIEGE

UNDER SIEGE

JOSH McDOWELL & CHUCK KLEIN
WITH ED STEWART

WORD PUBLISHING
Dallas · London · Vancouver · Melbourne

Under Siege

Library of Congress Cataloging-in-Publication Data:
McDowell, Josh.
    Under siege / Josh McDowell and Chuck Klein with Ed
Stewart.
        p.   cm.
    Summary: Stories and follow-up material illustrate how
by committing oneself to God, we can live better Christian
lives.
    ISBN 0–8499–3363–3
    [1. Christian life—Fiction.] I. Klein, Chuck. II. Stewart, Ed.
III. Title.
PZ7.M478446Un 1992
[Fic]—dc20   92–10881
                                                           CIP
                                                           AC

2 3 4 9   LB   9 8 7 6 5 4 3 2 1

Printed in the United States of America

Contents

Acknowledgments   7

 1 Hit It!   9
 2 The Mutants of Subsector 477   22
 3 "It'll Blow Your Doors Off!"   37
 4 Blue-White Terror   49
 5 The Bag Lady's Revenge   63
 6 Commandos   77
 7 Heavy Artillery   90
 8 Turkey Day Flop   103
 9 More Than Just Friends   116
10 Bombs Away!   128
11 Gully-Washer   141
12 The Main Event   154
13 We've Just Begun to Fight   169
14 A Day to Remember   183

Appendix   195

Acknowledgments

This book has truly been a collaborative effort and we want to acknowledge the team that helped bring it into being. We want to acknowledge the tremendous influence that Dr. Bill Bright and the Campus Crusade for Christ leadership have had on formulating our biblical concepts of evangelism and that of the Holy Spirit. Without that influence over the years, this book would not have been possible. We are deeply grateful to Ed Stewart for his spiritual insights, creativity, commitment to Christ, skill, and God-given talents as he masterfully crafted the intriguing and compelling story of the youth group from Eisenhower High. We are indebted to the many prayer groups who upheld Ed and us in prayer as we labored to create this book. Thanks goes to Gary Sivewright, Mark Gilroy, and Randy Cloud of the Nazarene Youth Ministry; to Dann Spader, Dave Garda, and Mark Edwards of Sonlife Ministries; and to Mark Stephens and Nancy Wilson of Student Venture for their val-uable input in conceptualizing, molding, and shaping the book's content. Special thanks goes to Dann Spader for his deep commitment to this project, his vision to reach kids for Christ, and his gifted leadership in championing PowerLink nationally. We want to express appreciation to Bill Jones, Doug Bosler, and the students at Columbiana Bible College and Seminary for reading and giving valuable feedback from the first draft manuscript. Many thanks also go to Bob Hostetler for his expertise and writing skills as he brought the manuscript to final completion. And finally, we want to thank Dave Bellis who strategically planned and developed the entire PowerLink campaign and creatively conceptualized this book and made it a centerpiece of the campaign.

Josh McDowell
Chuck Klein

1

Hit It!

Will McConnell knew he wasn't the most uncoordinated fifteen-year-old guy in the world. After all, he could make his Macintosh computer do somersaults in response to his nimble-fingered skills. But at this moment he seemed out of his element. Plopped in the middle of Gilligan's Lake, he was struggling like crazy to make his arms and legs do what they were supposed to do.

Strapped to his feet were a pair of water skis that seemed as big as surfboards to him.

"Keep your skis together with the tips above water and the ski rope between them," youth leader Duane Cunningham had instructed Will while he was still in the boat. "Crouch behind your skis in the water, grab the handle with both hands, lean back a little, and yell, 'Hit it.' Then just let the boat pull you out."

Sounded simple enough to Will. He'd watched fellow sophomore Amber Lockwood do it. She got up on her first try—beautiful! But then Will thought Amber was beautiful at *anything* she tried. And there was Tony Ortiz, the big senior, Ike High's hunk of the century—at least as far as Amber was concerned. Tony was as good at skimming across the water on his own custom stunt ski as he was at slashing through holes in a defensive line. *I'm no Tony Ortiz,* Will thought as he cinched up his life vest before jumping into the warm water for his first attempt. *But if Amber can do it, I know I can do it.*

"Ready, Willie?" Tony yelled from the boat. Will hated being called Willie, especially by the hunk of the century, especially when the hunk was showing off his hunkness around Amber.

Will was suddenly aware that he was ready. He crouched behind the two ski tips that rose from the water like the prows of a pair of speedboats. Both hands gripped the handle, and the rope stretched taut between him and Duane's sleek, rumbling Bayliner inboard-outboard.

Will's heart abruptly jump-started. "Hit it!" he squawked. Duane jammed the throttle open, the Bayliner roared to life, and Will began to surge forward, pushing water in front of him like an overloaded barge.

At first, Will feared that the pull of the boat against the weight of the water in front of him was going to rip his arms off at the shoulders, but somehow he hung on. Then he imagined that his knees were going to explode as he fought to keep the quivering skis from using him for a human wishbone. But he managed to keep them together and slowly raise his body out of the water. *I'm up! I'm water-skiing!* Will thought, exulting.

To call what Will was doing water-skiing required a little imagination. He was bent over at the waist so that his torso, head, and arms were stretched out in a line parallel to the water. His wobbling knees, which banged together like cymbals with every bump, nearly touched his life vest at the chest.

It was a couple minutes before Will could relax his concentration enough to think about what he looked like. He winced as he pictured himself as Amber saw him from the back of the boat: scrawny white legs and arms gleaming in the late August sun, raspberry neon swimsuit flapping against his thighs, sandy brown hair flying wildly in the wind. Will suddenly hated himself for not having the athletic talent and body that Tony had and for not having a father to teach him the finer arts of football, basketball, and water-skiing.

So I'm a Christian and Tony's not—big deal, he thought recklessly. *How's a guy like me supposed to get Amber's attention with a guy like Tony around? I'd trade places with him in a second.*

Will's thought sent a chill through him despite the 90-degree temperature that had already evaporated the water on his skin. He quickly stuffed the thought deep inside and chanced a look at the boat.

Duane turned around and glanced at Will from the driver's seat, then raised his fist signaling Will's triumph. Will smiled. He could also see Tony's arm draped around Amber's shoulder as they huddled in the backseat watching him. Will stopped smiling. He hated seeing Tony wrapped around Amber. There was something about Amber that turned Will's insides to Jell-O. She was tall and slender, with shoulder-length black hair, dark, full eyebrows, and green eyes. Her tan body was accented by a modest but definitely flattering swimsuit.

"I love you, Amber Lockwood," he sighed.

Amber waved at Will with one hand while keeping a square black object up near her eyes.

"Oh, no! Not the video camera!" Will grumbled aloud. "I hate you, Amber Lockwood!"

He flinched at the thought of his gangly attempt at water-skiing being laughed at by millions of people on one of those home video shows. And in his precarious posture, one flinch was too many. In an instant his center of gravity shifted forward, his skis veered toward opposite shores, and he plunged headfirst into the boat's churning wake, sending the skis airborne behind him. Once underwater he remembered to let go of the rope, but not before the current had filled his nose and mouth with water and jerked his swimsuit down to his ankles.

Will popped to the surface, coughed out a mouthful of water, and grabbed a lung full of air before frantically ducking under again to pull up his suit. His hands found his ankles, but his swimsuit was gone. In his haste to come up for air he had kicked it off. He opened his eyes underwater to look for it. The glowing raspberry suit was sinking fast. Will made a frenzied swipe for it, but the life vest bobbed him to the surface while his trunks fluttered toward the bottom.

He bobbed and sputtered, squinting to locate the boat. The Bayliner had wheeled around and was headed toward him fast. Amber was hanging over the side aiming the camera right at him. Will realized that her video would become R-rated in a matter of seconds if he didn't act quickly. He could see the title clearly: "Full Moon at High Noon."

Will jerked his arms out of his life vest and pulled it quickly down to where his swimsuit had been, covering his whiter parts.

"Are you okay?" Duane asked as he cut the throttle and let the boat drift alongside him. Will nodded with a sheepish grin.

"You did great, Will," Amber sang, zooming in on him in the water. "But how did your life vest get . . . ?"

Tony interrupted her question with a burst of laughter. "Lose something, Willie? Keep rolling the camera, Amber. Ol' Willie's doing a little Christian skinny-dipping."

"Did you really lose your trunks out there, Will?" Amber gasped with true embarrassment, turning the camera away respectfully.

Will tugged at the life vest self-consciously to ensure maximum coverage.

"I guess I . . . er, when I fell I . . ." Will's feeble attempt at an explanation only made Amber, Tony, and Duane laugh harder. He felt his face turn the color of his departed swimsuit. He wished he had sunk to the bottom with it.

It didn't seem like anyone was paying much attention to Duane's talk at the campfire that night—except maybe Liz, his wife. After an energy-sapping day of sunning, swimming, and water-skiing and a dinner of charcoal-broiled burgers, corn on the cob, and too many fudge brownies, Will McConnell and his fourteen fellow campers stared blankly at the flames while the new youth leader at Westcastle Community Church tried to make a point about prayer or something.

Will squirmed, uncomfortable from the sting of sunburn on his face and shoulders. But he squirmed even more inside from his humiliation on the lake that afternoon. (Amber and the hunk had been all too willing to relate the embarrassing details, and everybody laughed at Will when they found out.) He scanned the faces of those perched statue-still on the big logs that surrounded the campfire.

What kind of a Christian group was this anyway? he thought. He didn't know these kids, not really. And they obviously didn't know him, or they wouldn't have made such fun of him today.

Will stared at Amber directly across the campfire from him. She was now sheathed to the knees in Tony's football jersey, and her satiny hair was stuffed into a baseball cap— also Tony's. Will and Amber had grown up in the same neighborhood. Will had had a crush on her ever since they won the three-legged race together at a Sunday school picnic when they were both eleven years old. But Amber grew up to be a rally girl in the eye of Ike's social whirlwind, and Will consoled himself by making his computer his best friend.

Several of the kids around the campfire tonight had begun attending Westcastle Community Church during Will's middle school years. There was Joy Akiyama, one of the tiniest, shyest girls Will had ever met. *Paint on the wall has more personality than she does,* Will quipped to himself.

Sitting next to Joy, quietly filling the cuff of her jeans with sand as she stared, oblivious, into the fire, was Jason Withers. Will realized that, even though he and Jason were friends, they had never had a serious conversation about anything. Life to Jason was a never-ending series of jokes and pranks. And some of his pranks were so inventive and bold, well, it was scary.

Will's eyes flitted around the circle until they fell on Darcelle Davis. She was a large-boned African-American girl with short frizzy hair and a smile right out of a toothpaste commercial. She was well liked and highly respected at Ike High as junior class vice-president and a member of the National Honor Society. As a reporter for the school newspaper, Darcelle had published several feature articles dealing with school issues from a Christian standpoint. She wrote so positively that few people objected to her stand.

Will had heard all his life that Christians should read the Bible and pray every day. But he had never known anyone who really did until he met Darcelle. Will was sure that, come the Rapture, it would only take God half a twinkling of an eye to change Darcelle; she already seemed perfect. Buster Todd, a senior sitting near Darcelle, was kind of a saint too. But since Buster had only been in Westcastle a year, Will didn't know him as well.

Will, Amber, Jason, Joy, Darcelle, and a few others had logged a lot of hours together in youth meetings and outings like this one. But after today Will wondered if he had any real friends among them. Until they had that "See You at the Pole" thing, they had always acted like strangers to each other around school—even now, most of them had little more time for their church friends than to wave and smile at them in the halls. Something about the whole situation seemed to be stuck sideways in Will tonight, and he didn't like how it felt.

And what about newcomers like Tony Ortiz, his friend and teammate Reggie Spencer, and Reggie's girlfriend,

Krystal Wayne? Everybody knew that they ran with the wild bunch at Ike: kids who were boozing, using, and cruising for sex. Tony had only come on the campout to be close to Amber. Reggie and Krystal had never attended church. Reggie came to be with Tony, and Krystal went everywhere Reggie went. *What were crude dudes like these doing on a Christian outing?* Will wondered spitefully.

Later that night when Will climbed into the pup tent he shared with Jason Withers, his rough-edged thoughts and feelings were still banging around inside him.

"I don't think Ortiz and Spencer and Krystal should be here," Will said in the darkness after he had endured a stream of Jason's corny jokes. "I think they're just bringing our group down." Will didn't know if his attempt at a serious conversation would fly with Jason, but he had to try.

"Bringing our group down from where?" Jason retorted cynically. "In case you haven't noticed, even without Tony, Reggie, and Krystal around, this group isn't exactly a blazing success at being Christian. Half the kids are fooling around with stuff they shouldn't be messing with. They just hide it better than pagans like Tony and Amber."

"Wait a minute," Will objected. "Tony may be a pagan, but Amber's a Christian. I've known her a lot longer than you have."

"Well, she's sure spending a lot of time with the pagans these days, and I don't think it's because she's on some holy mission to convert them. I know you've got goo-goo eyes for her, but forget it, man. She's a big girl now. If she wants to play in the major leagues with guys like Tony, you're not going to stop her."

Will realized that he wasn't going to get any sympathy from Jason about Amber.

"What do you know about Spencer and Krystal?" he said, changing the subject.

"He's a tough guy—offensive lineman, wrestler. He's also quite an all-star with the brew. And I hear he's done about everything with Krystal that a guy can do—but then what guy on the football team hasn't?" Jason chortled wickedly.

Will gave up on getting a serious opinion out of him. They lay quietly for less than two minutes before both of them were asleep.

Will couldn't tell if it was his sunburn or his heartburn from too many brownies that woke him in the middle of the night. He was too hot and his stomach was queasy, so he scooted up to stick his head outside the tent and breathe the fresh air. Except for Jason's steady breathing, the softly moonlit night around his tent was quiet. Will looked across the campfire area to where the girls' tents were pitched next to the trees that bordered their beach campsite. He had just made out Amber and Darcelle's tent when he thought he saw something move. He quickly slid back into his tent and peeked out the flap to see a tall, slender figure in an oversized football jersey emerge from the tent and creep away toward the beach.

Amber! Will thought as his heart began thundering behind his sternum. Then an idea crashed in on him so quickly that he reacted to it before he really thought about it. *I'm never going to get a chance to talk to you during the day when Tony is around,* he convinced himself as he slid into his jeans and Nikes. *I need to warn you about hanging out with Ortiz and his friends. And a quiet midnight walk along the beach is the perfect opportunity.*

Will watched from behind his tent until Amber reached the shoreline and began walking alongside it. He moved to the edge of the trees without making a sound and followed her in the shadows with about a hundred yards of sand separating them.

Will was ready to come out of the trees and call to her, when Amber turned away from the shoreline and began angling toward the trees. Will stopped abruptly and slid into the darkest shadow he could find. *Where are you going,*

Amber? he demanded silently, perplexed. *There's nothing in these trees except crickets and . . .*

Suddenly Will spied a flicker of light in the darkness about fifty yards ahead, just at the spot in the trees Amber seemed to be walking toward. He waited until Amber had almost reached the trees, then he began moving forward slowly. His heart was pounding so loudly in his ears he was afraid Amber would hear it. Something was going on here, something he probably wasn't supposed to know about. He crept forward. Soon he heard voices.

He peered cautiously between the trees until he could make out the dim light of a small flashlight aimed at a sawed-off tree stump. The silhouettes behind the light were very familiar to Will. He had studied the four shapes from the other side of the campfire during Duane's talk. It was Tony, Reggie, Krystal, and Amber. They were huddled together on a log around a stack of beer cans on the stump.

"I knew you wouldn't want to miss out on the fun," Will heard Tony say to Amber, handing her a can and pulling the tab. Amber took the can, but Tony, who appeared a little unsteady on his feet, wrapped his arms around her before she could take a sip.

"And the fun's just beginning, right Krystal?" Reggie said, slurring his words slightly. Krystal giggled a response that Will couldn't understand, then the two of them fell together in a long kiss. Even in the dim light Will's eyes were shocked wide open when he saw Reggie slide his hands inside Krystal's shirt.

They're drunk, all three of them! Will complained angrily to himself. *And Tony's dragging Amber right into the middle of it!*

Tony kissed Amber lightly on the cheek, then on the mouth. Amber cooperated, but Will thought—or at least hoped—that she wasn't wholehearted about it. Tony drank from Amber's can and encouraged her to take a sip. She did but quickly put her hand to her mouth as if gagging on the stuff.

Tony took the can from Amber's hand. "This is what you really need, Baby," he said as he folded her into his arms and kissed her forcefully on the mouth. Amber's arms reached up and embraced him willingly.

Will had seen enough. He had to get away from there before he exploded and Tony and Reggie pounded him. He backtracked slowly and silently through the trees to the beach, then jogged toward camp. He was mad at Tony for taking advantage of Amber, and he was mad at Amber for letting him. He was mad at himself for being such a wimp that he couldn't stand up to guys like Tony. And he was mad at Duane Cunningham for letting kids get drunk and make out in the woods and for letting them humiliate him for a simple thing like losing a swimsuit in the lake.

Will was even mad at God. *You'd better do something about Tony Ortiz, God,* he fumed inside as he jogged in the moonlight. *You're letting Amber get sucked under by dirtbags like Tony, Reggie, and Krystal. You'd just better do something, God, or I'll* . . . Will suddenly realized that it was pointless to try to threaten God.

By the time he slipped silently into his sleeping bag, Will's anger had boiled over into embarrassing tears. For the first time in weeks he tried to pray—*really* pray. He wanted to convince God that He should rescue Amber. But his fragile concentration kept getting interrupted by painful childhood memories of his father loading suitcases into the car and driving away. And every time he tried to breathe Amber's name in prayer he started to wonder how it would be to hold her next to him, kiss her, and . . . confused, distracted, and suddenly exhausted, Will fell asleep.

Had he stayed awake a few minutes longer he might have seen Amber sneaking back into camp alone. She was crying too.

The Inside Story: Running on Empty

Typical Christian group? Perhaps. Maybe it's even like your youth group or Christian club. Oh, you may not go water-skiing at Gilligan's Lake, but you do stuff together: pizza parties, roller skating, car washes, summer camps, winter retreats, and so on. And you may not have a real, live youth leader. But it's likely that some adults are around to offer advice and support.

You also probably have a cast of characters not too different from those in this story. You may have a few clowns or pranksters like Jason Withers—real performers. They can't seem to get very serious about anything, but you wouldn't want to have a party without them. You may have a few Joy Akiyamas who attend but rarely speak or act up. You may have kids like Will McConnell, brainy, computer types who ruin the grading curve, and guys like Buster Todd, who are happiest when they have something to tear apart, tinker with, and put back together. Then there are the Amber Lockwoods, girls and guys who are better looking and more popular than really seems fair. And we've probably missed some of the types in your group.

You may compare your group to this "typical" group in another way. You have kids at different levels in their relationship with Christ. Hopefully there are some like Darcelle Davis and Buster Todd. These kids are not without warts, but from the way they live you can tell that Jesus Christ is very important to them. You may also attract kids like Tony, Reggie, and Krystal from time to time. They aren't Christians at all, and they rarely pretend that they are. Their main interest is fun, and if your group offers it, they'll show up once in awhile.

In between these two extremes is the well-populated middle. Like Will, Amber, and some of their friends, these kids have trusted Christ sometime in the past, but most of the time they are occupied with a lot of other concerns, like what other people think of them, what they're going to do this weekend, or how they're going to solve their problems at home. It's not that they don't think God is important. It's just that they don't take time to get more serious about a relationship with Christ—until a big problem comes along.

But there's another way to look at the members of a typical youth group. It has to do with something they *all* have in common, whether they're eggheads or jocks, wallflowers or rally girls, leaders or followers, committed Christians or pagans. It's probably the way your group most closely identifies with Will and Amber's group.

Everybody has needs. No matter what your level of spiritual maturity and commitment or what activities you're involved in, you carry with you some degree of inner pain. Why? Because you have God-given physical, emotional, social, and spiritual needs that aren't being fully met. Like Will McConnell, you may be hurting because you don't feel loved and accepted by your parents or friends. Like Amber Lockwood, you may be struggling inside because you don't really know who you are or because you can't seem to find satisfaction or purpose in your life. Or, like Tony, Reggie, and Krystal, you may be hurting because you've made some poor choices in life, and now you're caught in a vicious cycle of trying to escape from your guilt.

The crazy thing about needs and hurts is that most kids don't want to *look* like they have them, so they hide them behind a false front that conveys, "Everything's cool, no problems, I've got it all together." That's why Will wanted to look good in front of Amber on water skis. And that's why Amber accepted Tony's invitation to a midnight rendezvous in the trees. Each of them in their own way is trying to look good when inside they are feeling bad.

Hidden needs are not just hidden, they're unfulfilled. Even if you don't recognize the need, you still yearn for love, acceptance, satisfaction, and freedom in your life. And putting on a mask or trying to act like you've got your life under control doesn't fill the emptiness. So you may attempt to fill your needs by submerging yourself in efforts to achieve grades, status, or popularity. You may try to drown your needs and hurts under a tidal wave of diversions—music, movies, parties, video games, cruising, shopping, carousing. Or you may simply try to dull your inner pain with addictions to food, alcohol, drugs, or sex. If you are involved in some kind of behavior you can't control, whether it's good or bad, it may be a futile attempt to fill the emptiness in your life.

The great tragedy of kids' spending all their time and energy trying to satisfy their inner emptiness is that they don't have any time or energy left to do what God created them to do: love Him, enjoy Him, and share Him with others. But, of course, such a tragedy is not an accident, as a visit to a smoky cavern somewhere far below the community of Westcastle will illustrate.

2

The Mutants of Subsector 477

Demon Ratsbane hopped and waddled through the maze of crowded, smoldering caverns far below Westcastle's sunlit streets. His wart-covered fingers clutched a tattered folder stuffed with documents. He was a mutant, like all those who had been thrown out of heaven with Satan so many eons ago. In his attempt to mock the Enemy, the evil one had refashioned each of his followers using a jumble of body parts crudely copied from the Enemy's originals. Ratsbane had been stuck with the torso, stubby arms, and gangly legs of an oversized toad and the grotesquely enlarged black head of a carpenter ant.

Ratsbane reached a fork in the tunnel and fumed over which way to go. He grabbed a passing maintenance runt bearing a hideous combination of rodent and fish features.

"Which way to Subsector 477?" Ratsbane croaked.

The sneering little creature spat at him, then reluctantly pointed a fin toward the tunnel on the left. Ratsbane flipped the runt aside with a curse and continued his journey.

After several more snarling, spitting confrontations, Ratsbane finally found his way to Subsector 477. He turned off the main tunnel and waddled through a rugged archway into a huge workroom that pounded his antennae with noise.

"Where's the sector boss?" he snarled to a runt he grabbed by the tail.

"Maledictus? Right up there," the creature said, pointing to a pile of boulders. "On the tower."

After several minutes of arduous climbing, Ratsbane stood in the imposing presence of a gigantic, coiled python with a majestic swan's head. "The serpent mutants get all the good jobs," Ratsbane grunted to himself.

"Lord Maledictus," he addressed the swan-python while bowing, "Demon Ratsbane at your service. I'm the new PIT operator you requested." Ratsbane's subservient demeanor was nothing but show, of course. Inside he cowered to no creature below the Prince of Darkness himself, even though he had never met him in person.

Maledictus hissed lowly, then lashed out and snatched Ratsbane's folder with his beak, painfully nicking the toadant's webbed hand in the process. The supervisor leafed hurriedly through the file. "Have you ever worked in the Temptation division before, you despicable mutant?" he growled.

"No, sir. I've been in the Torment division since shortly after the Fall. But I have a distinguished record both as an apparatus operator and a supervisor at that level, commended by Prince Satan himself."

"Scorch your record in Torment!" Maledictus screamed, tossing the file into the smoke-filled air. The pages fluttered to the ground around the tower. "It's a different ball game at this level. Down there by the Lake of Fire you already have them in your grasp. They're dead and buried, yours to play with for eternity. But up here they're still kicking, still able to defect to the Enemy. One little oversight on the PIT apparatus and a chain reaction could erupt, leading to a revolution on the surface."

Maledictus lowered his grotesque head so that his razor-sharp beak was within inches of Ratsbane's bulbous black eyes. "The only reason you're here, you ugly excuse for a demon, is because we're a little short-handed in dealing with some of the Enemy's rebels in Subsector 477. Any slip-ups on your part will be hazardous to your career. Do I make myself clear, Demon Ratsbane?"

Ratsbane returned the swan-python's ferocious, intimidating glare with one of his own. "Maledictus, once I get the hang of the PIT apparatus and am commended again by the Great Satan for my efforts, it's your job that will be in jeopardy."

Maledictus blinked, surprised at the gall of the stumpy little mutant. They stared at each other, their eyes pulsing with hatred for each other.

"The PIT apparatus for Subsector 477 is down there," the swan-python hissed at last, motioning toward one of numerous openings in the wall of the large cave. "You'll be at the keyboard with Marplot and Stygios. Tell Marplot—the big one—that I sent you. Now get out of my sight."

The PIT cave was much larger than Ratsbane expected, and the famed Prime-evil Impulse Transducer itself was more immense and complex than anything he'd worked on in Torment. It had the appearance of a gigantic pipe organ made of multi-colored polished stone.

The PIT's horseshoe-shaped keyboard was comprised of hundreds of buttons, levers, and dials that blinked and glowed in the dark, smoky cave. Above the keyboard was a series of video monitors flickering characters and images in a ghostly greenish-gray. And reaching up from behind the console were the "pipes": hundreds of stone conduits of various widths and colors that stretched into the craggy ceiling of the cave. Each conduit carried a cluster of cables transmitting invisible impulses from the PIT to the targets of Subsector 477 above: the students of Eisenhower Senior High School in the community of Westcastle (for tens of thousands of miles in every direction, Prime-evil Impulse Transducers like this one, manned by Satan's goons, terrorized the population of the entire planet).

As he waddled toward the PIT, Ratsbane could make out the figures of two demon mutants working furiously at the massive keyboard. One was much larger than he—the body of a wild hog and the head of a crocodile. The other was a beaver with a pelican's head.

"Marplot?" he called loudly to the crocodile-hog above the whirring static of the transmitting PIT.

Marplot turned to him reluctantly while Stygios the pelican-beaver continued to pound the buttons and twist the dials. "What do you want?" the large mutant growled.

"Name is Ratsbane. Maledictus sent me. I'm here to work at the keyboard. You are to show me how this apparatus works."

Marplot grunted. "It's about time we got some help. But you'll have to learn the system by watching us. No time to give you a seminar. If we fall behind, Maledictus will have our heads." Then the large mutant turned back to the blinking keyboard and resumed his frantic work.

Ratsbane climbed the scaffolding that gave smaller mutants like him and Stygios better access to the controls. Standing between the two of them, Ratsbane watched with fascination as the two PIT operators worked.

"It's really quite simple under normal conditions," Marplot called out above the whirs, crackles, and hums coming from the console. "The cables from the Prime-evil Impulse Transducer go up the conduit through the ceiling and permeate our entire subsector. These lines—which are invisible on the surface, of course—are attached to our captives up there. Our job is to keep transmitting the blinding impulses necessary to keep them as captives and prevent them from joining the rebellion."

Marplot couldn't stifle a fiendish cackle at the thought of the students in Westcastle groping purposely through life under the influence of the PIT.

"But what about the rebels, those students who have already escaped the blinding influence of the PIT?" Ratsbane asked.

"The sighted ones! Bah!" Marplot snorted with disgust as he worked the buttons and levers with his hog hoofs. "It's horrible when their PIT lines are severed by the Enemy's brigadiers and they can suddenly see. When our blinding impulses back up on those broken lines, we have conduits and control panels exploding all over the place." Marplot shuddered at the thought. Ratsbane noticed that many of the stone panels on the keyboard and conduits to the ceiling had been crudely repaired.

"Once they rebel the PIT can no longer keep them in the dark as it once did," Marplot continued. "But, luckily, many of them don't realize how free they are. So we continue to transmit impulses through the severed lines all around them. You'd be surprised how gullible these wretched believers are to the blind spots we use to surround them. That's the key to snuffing out the rebellion, of course. The more they stumble around in the darkness of their old ideas and ways, the more difficult it is for them to influence the other captives to rebel and seek freedom."

"Is the PIT responsible for all the dark thoughts and deeds these miserable creatures entertain?" Ratsbane asked.

"Of course not!" Marplot rumbled, incensed at Ratsbane's stupidity. "Thanks to the Great Satan's success in Eden, the fallen world and all its delights surround them with blinding temptations, distractions, and diversions. I mean, why clog up the PIT lines transmitting thoughts of illicit sex and violence all the time when television programs and rentable videos do it for us?

"And they're all related to Adam, you know. Our captives have an old fleshly nature that is inherited from him. They live in sin and selfishness quite well without much help from us. And even the rebels whose eyes have been opened are still plagued by old, dark habits that often cause them to think and act more like captives than liberated rebels. Luckily, many of them have no idea that the Enemy has given them a new nature, and they haven't figured out that His Spirit lives in them to give them power over the darkness.

"No, Ratsbane, we can't take credit for everything. But the world, the flesh, and the devil working together can crank out a flood of debilitating darkness."

"What kinds of impulses can this contraption transmit?" Ratsbane asked as he surveyed the jumble of controls before him.

"There are millions of combinations, Ratsbane," the crocodile-hog demon boasted, "but they all come back to this." Marplot tapped his hoof on a large, purple-glowing, well-worn button on the panel marked ME. "Self-centeredness blocks out more light than almost anything. That's what makes the old fleshly nature so effective for us. Whatever else you do, you must tempt those wretched captives and rebels to think of themselves first. Blast them with impulses of self-gratification, self-pity, self-everything. As long as they're selfishly focused on 'me,' they won't have much time for the Enemy or anyone else."

"Marplot!" Stygios squawked loudly through his pelican beak. "Alert on 8860!" Marplot rapidly punched in the coordinates, and a fuzzy image fluttered onto the monitor directly in front of Ratsbane.

"Aha! You again!" Marplot snarled at the figure on the screen. Ratsbane leaned closer, his huge black eyes wide open and his antennae erect. He could see a skinny, sandy-haired teenage boy lying in a sleeping bag inside a pup tent. His eyes were slightly moist, and he appeared to be mouthing a prayer.

"So we caught you trying to pray for that girl again, eh?" Marplot growled. Then he turned his head slightly toward Ratsbane while keeping his blazing crocodile eyes on the monitor. "Watch this, Ratsbane. I'll give you a firsthand look at how the Prime-evil Impulse Transducer can effectively beat down this sniveling little wimp's concern for a rebel girl we have on the ropes."

Marplot's hooves moved swiftly over the console snapping switches and twisting dials. "This kid, who calls himself Will McConnell, had his PIT lines severed as a child. Fortunately, he's not been much trouble to us since then. He goes to church and hangs out with his Christian group. But we keep pounding him about being the cause of his father leaving his mother when he was five. As a result he's been so full of pain that he often wonders if the Enemy even cares about him. So we just have to punch the ME button on him a few times a day, throw in a little anger, guilt, and self-pity once in awhile, and he can't think of anyone but 'poor little me.'"

Marplot directed his full attention to Will's image on the monitor. "So now you think little Amber Lockwood is too sweet to be gobbled up by that big, bad unbeliever, Tony Ortiz. And you think your wimpy little last-resort prayer might make a difference. Well, how can you pray when you're thinking about your dad leaving you?" The demon pushed a couple of levers and pounded blinking buttons marked SELF-PITY and GUILT. A stone conduit warbled, howled, and shimmied as the transmission was sent. Will's lips stopped moving.

"And how can you think about the girl's soul when you're drooling over her body? You want her even more than Ortiz does, don't you?" Marplot giggled wickedly as he spun two more dials and repeatedly punched the blazing red LUST button along with the blazing ME button. As the boy on the monitor was trying to fight his sudden alarming thoughts he fell asleep.

Marplot uttered a raspy sigh of contentment and turned to Ratsbane with a fiendish crocodile grin. "That's how it's done, my friend. Keep pounding them with the PIT and watch them crumble under the pressure."

Bam! Crackle! Bam! Crackle! Crackle! One of the conduits suddenly shattered, showering the three demons with sparks and jagged chunks of stone. Even hardened Ratsbane was startled.

"Alert on 989!" Stygios squealed with alarm. Marplot had the problem on the monitor in seconds. He screamed a bitter curse, and Ratsbane leaned closer to the console to watch. The static-speckled screen revealed two teenaged girls in a small tent. One of them, a slender girl with dark, silky hair, was sobbing. The other girl, black-skinned, had her arm around the first girl and was praying for her.

"I just knew that midnight drinking party in the woods wouldn't work out right!" Marplot spat, furiously trying to jam Darcelle Davis's prayer with a combination of impulses. "That jerk Ortiz failed to get her drunk, and he was too drunk himself to seduce her properly. So he just pawed all over her until he scared her away. Now she has awakened that praying fanatic in her tent and told her everything. We're losing ground with that little twit Amber Lockwood, Stygios. More power, give me more power!"

Ratsbane watched intently for the next hour as Marplot and Stygios pounded out countless combinations on the buttons, dials, switches, and levers to break up the midnight prayer meeting. They blasted Amber with thoughts of pride, trying to convince her that she could handle her own problems. They badgered Darcelle with guilt. "Who are you to pray for Amber?" Marplot taunted. "You were in worse shape than she is." But sparks continued to spurt from the fractured conduit and splash around the console. Then Marplot watched in agony as a third female joined Amber and Darcelle in the tent: Liz Cunningham, the youth leader's wife. And her prayers caused another loud split in the conduit.

When the meeting finally broke up and the girls went to sleep, Marplot flew into a rage while a couple of maintenance runts tried to repair the damages. He screamed at Stygios for not increasing the PIT's power quickly enough and lashed out at Ratsbane for breaking his concentration.

When Marplot's rage had diminished to mild seething, he turned to his new recruit. "This is why you're here, Demon Ratsbane. Problems like these have been occurring more frequently in our subsector since they took over the leadership of those Christians at Eisenhower High." Marplot jabbed a hoof toward a still photo on one of the monitors of Duane and Liz Cunningham.

"They are dangerous radicals in the Enemy's ranks, Ratsbane. They pray hard, study hard, love hard, and work hard for Him. They've only been in Westcastle six months, but they've already upset the status quo of the Christian students. The ripple effect of their antics could disrupt our entire subsector.

"Your orders are to bring an end to the spiritual uprising in this small group. Stygios and I have fourteen hundred other youths to monitor at Eisenhower High School. As you've already seen, this contemptible little enemy group and their pesky leaders need constant attention. Research their weaknesses and start tearing them to shreds. Lord Maledictus will not tolerate failure, and neither will I!"

The next several hours in Subsector 477 were rather quiet as most of the students in Westcastle slept. While Marplot and Stygios busied themselves on the console, Ratsbane pulled up the files of the offensive rebels. His sharp eyes and lightning-fast hands helped him quickly adapt to the PIT apparatus. And his diabolical drive fired him with determination to squash this group of upstarts.

Ratsbane learned that the majority of those attending the weekend campout at Gilligan's Lake were like Will McConnell. They were rebels all right, but they were harmless rebels, more susceptible to worldly attractions, fleshly habits, and prime-evil impulses than to the Enemy's Spirit.

He reviewed the files of some of the group's toothless believers.

- Will McConnell, sophomore, the computer whiz: blames himself for his parents' break-up; feels rejected by both of them as well as his peers; has difficulty believing that the Enemy can accept him either.
- Amber Lockwood, sophomore, the rally girl: grew up under strict thou-shalt-not parents; is experimenting with some of the "shalt nots" to see what she is missing; has difficulty forgiving herself and accepting the Enemy's forgiveness.
- Joy Akiyama, junior, the wallflower: raised by adoptive parents who beat her and molested her; deals with her pain and anger by burying them deep inside; afraid to do anything for fear that the Enemy will hurt her as her parents did.
- Jason Withers, sophomore, the clown: good parents but they often work long hours, leaving him home alone; is addicted to video games and cable smut; gets attention through his jokes and pranks; feels he can't perform well enough to earn the Enemy's love.

Ratsbane pulled up and reviewed the files of three students on the campout whose PIT lines were still intact:

- Tony Ortiz, senior, the jock: urged by his father to fight for what he wants in life; intent on setting records for yardage gained, kegs consumed, and girls seduced; thinks anyone who serves the Enemy is a wimp.
- Reggie Spencer, senior, the follower: parents divorced— father is an alcoholic, mother sleeps around; wants to rise above his parents' example but lacks the personal discipline; easily influenced by the wrong crowd.
- Krystal Wayne, junior, the self-abuser: rebelled against the image of an older sister to establish her own

identity; lives fast and loose; has used and dealt hard stuff and turned a few tricks to support her habit.

Ratsbane growled hatefully as he pulled up the files of the handful of radicals who were the reason behind his reassignment to Subsector 477:

- Duane Cunningham, age twenty-six, carpenter and volunteer youth leader: committed activist for the Enemy during college; feels called to incite spiritual rebellion among youth.

- Liz Cunningham, age twenty-five, part-time sales clerk, full-time wife: met Duane in a rebel prayer group at college; special interest in helping girls develop into radicals for the Enemy.

- Darcelle Davis, junior, the smiling student leader: lives with her mother, never knew her father; had an abortion and a miscarriage during the eighth grade; became a rebel radical at a Christian summer conference before her freshman year.

- Buster Todd, junior, Army "brat" and mechanical genius: grew up in a strong rebel family; moved to Westcastle as a sophomore; talks about the Enemy incessantly.

Ratsbane was just about to enter some personal notes on the files when Stygios squawked with alarm, "Check 5454, Ratsbane!" As he punched in the coordinates he could see from the corners of his bulging eyes that Marplot and Stygios were watching to see how he would handle his first alert.

The monitor blinked to life in front of him. It was morning at the lake. Two figures were readying the boat for a day of skiing. As they worked, Duane Cunningham was explaining to Tony Ortiz that he knew all about the party in the woods. The youth leader was kind but firm as he told Tony that such behavior was inappropriate for their outing. Then Duane began to turn the conversation toward the Enemy. A couple of conduits above Ratsbane began to rattle as Tony appeared to be listening.

Ratsbane's wart-covered hands flew into action. He pounded the ME button furiously on Tony's circuit. He spun several dials and jerked at a couple of levers, causing the conduits to throb and hum with impulses. "That idiot can't help you reach your goals, Tony," he hissed to the image on the screen as he worked. "Don't let him shove any of the Enemy's garbage down your throat." Tony began to fidget as Duane talked. Then he began to argue with the youth pastor defiantly.

A momentary flash of pride gripped the youth leader. Ratsbane took advantage of his weakness by flooding the severed lines near Duane Cunningham with combinations of impatience, anger, and self-righteousness. Duane resisted admirably, and a bright shower of sparks caused Marplot and Stygios to duck for cover.

But Ratsbane kept fueling the discussion with fiery impulses until it erupted into a shouting match on the screen. Finally, Tony stomped away cursing as Duane stood watching, flushed with anger. The sparks stopped abruptly.

Ratsbane stepped back from the keyboard and turned to his coworkers with a devilish grin. "Very good, Ratsbane," Marplot said, obviously impressed. "Very good indeed."

"The best is yet to come," the new PIT operator cackled confidently.

The Inside Story:
Chained in the Darkness

The account of Ratsbane and the Prime-evil Impulse Transducer is fiction, of course. But the sobering reality it illustrates comes right out of God's Word. Here's the way it really is.

First, before you received Christ and committed your life to Him, you were a captive of sin and Satan. You were blind to the truth about Jesus Christ. Describing the prior condition of a group of believers in Ephesus, Paul wrote: "You were dead in your transgressions and sins, in which you used to live when you followed the ways of this world and of the ruler of the kingdom of the air, the spirit who is now at work in those who are disobedient. All of us also lived among them at one time, gratifying the cravings of our sinful nature and following its desires and thoughts" (Ephesians 2:1–3).

There were no PIT lines attached to you as there are to Tony, Reggie, and Krystal in this story. But the world, the flesh, and the devil jerked you around just as surely as if you were chained to them. (If you haven't trusted Christ, you are still the prisoner of Satan and your sin. But don't worry—there's good news ahead.)

Second, before you committed your life to Christ, you were the hopeless, helpless victim of what is called your sinful or fleshly nature. And this sinful nature cannot meet your needs or ease your hurts. It just makes them worse. "When your old nature was still active," wrote Paul, "sinful desires were at work within you, making you want to do whatever God said not to, and producing sinful deeds, the rotting fruit of death" (Romans 7:5 TLB).

Satan, your captor, was intent on making your life miserable in every way. Jesus said of him: "The thief [Satan] comes only to steal and kill and destroy" (John 10:10). Satan and sin engineered the dissatisfaction, pain, guilt, and frustration that characterized your life without Christ.

Third, the moment you trusted Christ and committed your life to Him, you were set free from your captivity to Satan and sin. "Therefore," Paul declared, "there is now no condemnation for those who are in Christ Jesus, because through Christ Jesus the law of the Spirit of life set me free from the law of sin and death" (Romans 8:1–2). Your "PIT lines" were severed and the power of your old nature to control you was broken. You are free. You are no longer under the control of your former masters—Satan and your sinful nature.

"But," you might be saying, "it's not that simple. My life doesn't always run smoothly since I trusted Christ. I'm still tempted—sometimes a lot. And I don't always live like I know a Christian should. I blow it!"

True, even though you are free from sin's control, Satan, the world around you, and the habits of your old nature may be working together to keep you from enjoying the freedom, peace, and satisfaction of knowing Christ. Even Paul experienced the frustration of struggling with defeated enemies who were intent on keeping him tangled in his sinful ways. "When I want to do good," he admitted, "evil is right there with me. For in my inner being I delight in God's law; but I see another law at work in the members of my body, waging war against the law of my mind and making me a prisoner of the law of sin at work within my members. What a wretched man I am! Who will rescue me from this body of death?" (Romans 7:21–24).

Paul was really discouraged. Have you felt the frustration he agonized about? Perhaps you're so bogged down by guilt and pain from old habits that you wonder, "What's the benefit of being a Christian anyway? I'm just as miserable as I ever was."

Or maybe you've never trusted Christ, and you've tried all kinds of substances or experiences to try to ease the hurt and fill the emptiness in your life.

God didn't create you to go through life feeling frustrated and guilty. He wants you to be satisfied and full. How do you get that way? Well, a group of kids at Ike High are about to find out.

3

"It'll Blow Your Doors Off!"

Will had decided not to attend the party at Duane and Liz's. It was the last Friday night before the start of the fall semester. He was looking forward to spending the evening flying from Westcastle to Chicago on his Mac's flight simulator to the accompaniment of Wounded Twinkie's latest album. Besides, they were going to show the tapes from last weekend's campout. Will wasn't exactly thrilled about an instant replay of his losing his swimsuit, especially with everyone there to laugh at him again. And he was still smarting inside from seeing Amber involved in that make-out session in the woods. He was afraid the party would just rub salt in his wounds.

But then Darcelle, the publicity committee, had called.

"Don't forget the meeting. We're having banana splits, you know, and I guarantee this meeting is going to blow your doors off!"

"Why? What do you mean?"

"Never mind, you'll find out. See you there, right?"

Will's reasons for not attending were suddenly outvoted by his addiction to banana splits and his curiosity about Darcelle's secret. He could delay his take-off until 10:00 P.M.

"Right. See you there," he said.

As Will walked the four blocks from the apartment he shared with his mother to the complex where the Cunninghams lived, some of the memories from the campout came back to him. Of course, he would never forget following Amber into the trees and watching Tony wrap her in his gorilla arms. Will hadn't told a soul about his midnight spy mission; he didn't want to be labeled a Peeping Tom. But somebody had obviously blabbed about it to Duane. *Wow, was he steamed!* Will thought, recalling Duane's confrontation with Tony the next morning that had escalated into a shouting match. Will hadn't thought that Christian youth leaders had tempers.

Will also acknowledged to himself that the last campfire of the trip was something he would long remember. The only person missing from the circle on Saturday night was Tony, who had packed up and driven home in his own car shortly after his argument with Duane. Amber, Reggie, and Krystal had stayed—why, Will didn't know. He thought for sure they would want to get out too before the rumors about their late-night activities were confirmed.

Duane had started his campfire talk that night by apologizing to the group for losing his temper with Tony. He told how he had confessed his outburst to the Lord and knew God's forgiveness. He also apologized to Tony before he left. Everybody around the campfire was suddenly hanging on Duane's every word—including Amber, Reggie, and Krystal.

Then Duane had told a story that had stuck with Will all week. It was about a young woman who was stopped by a policeman for driving fifty-five in a thirty-five mile-per-hour zone. When she appeared before the judge she admitted that she was guilty. The judge fined her $100, then took off his robe, stepped down from his bench and paid the fine out of his own wallet. The judge was also the girl's father, Duane explained. She had broken the law, and as a good judge he had to penalize her. But he loved her so much that he was willing to pay the fine for her.

Duane said that the story illustrated God's love for people. As a just God, He had to penalize us for our sin, and the punishment sin brings is death. But as our loving Father He paid the penalty for us and offered us a life of freedom by sending Jesus to die in our place. The story made Will feel strangely warm, like a friendly campfire was glowing inside him. And that inner fire had somehow pushed Will's embarrassment and concern for Amber into the shadows for a few days.

"Hey, Will, good to see you! Glad you came!" Duane said at the door. Will smiled and nodded, then quickly scanned the living room. The whole gang was there hungrily scarfing up monster banana splits. Jason waved at him in between oversized scoops, and Darcelle smiled one of her smiles. Tony, Amber, Reggie, and Krystal were absent, as Will had expected. He doubted that Tony would ever show up at one of their activities again, and he wondered if Amber had finally bailed out of the group to be with him.

With a huge banana split under his belt, Will was anxious to get through the campout videos and see if Darcelle's secret could really blow his doors off. The group huddled around the television and laughed and hooted at themselves on videotape. Will actually found himself enjoying the rise and fall of his brief water-skiing career. And when he appeared on the screen wearing a life vest where his swimsuit should be, Will realized why everybody had laughed at him, and this time Will laughed too. It really *was* funny.

About halfway through the show he heard Liz greet somebody at the front door, then the late arriver sat down behind him on the carpet.

"Hi, Will," Amber whispered as she tapped him on the shoulder. He was so startled to hear Amber's voice that he jerked around as if somebody had dropped ice down his shirt. All the questions about Amber that had been crouching in a corner of his mind since the night in the trees jumped into his throat and stuck there: *Did you get drunk with Tony? Did you have sex with him? Have you given up on church and the youth group and God to join the wild bunch?* But all he could force himself to say was, "What are you doing here?"

Somehow Amber read the concern in Will's voice.

"You'll find out," she answered with a warm, sweet smile.

After the campout videos Duane sat down on a short stool beside the television. "We had a great campout, didn't we?" he began. Everybody hummed their agreement. "But as most of you know, some things happened last weekend that weren't exactly on the program." The room became very quiet. Will could feel several pairs of eyes flick in the direction of the girl sitting directly behind him. *Don't tell me Duane's going to ream her out in front of everybody!* he moaned inside. *Can this be Darcelle's great surprise? I knew I shouldn't have come.* He subconsciously sat a little taller to shield Amber from the stares aimed her way.

Duane continued.

"Some of the things that happened were bad things, obviously Satan's attempt to ruin the good things God had planned for our trip. But I want you to hear from three people who discovered last weekend that God can take bad things and turn them into good things—even great things—for Himself." Then Duane turned toward Will and nodded.

Will's heart suddenly jumped into his throat. *Are you looking at me? Do you expect me to say something?* Will gasped inside. Then he heard rustling behind him. Amber got up, walked to Duane's side, and sat down on a stool he had pulled next to his. Will was relieved that Duane had been nodding at Amber instead of him. But he was also stunned, wondering why she was being asked to address the group after what she had done with Tony. He leaned closer, eyes and ears wide open.

Amber spoke slowly and quietly, not at all like you might expect from a rally girl.

"As you all know, I've been a Christian most of my life. But I've always thought that God was kind of a kill-joy. So last year I decided that I didn't want Him standing in the way of my fun. I started trying some things that my parents had always told me were wrong, things I knew were wrong. I've been playing the role of the nice Christian girl at church. But I really haven't been very nice." Amber dropped her head, and Will could tell she was fighting back tears. Darcelle, sitting nearby, placed a comforting hand on Amber's knee.

Amber sighed deeply, then continued. "Most of you have heard by now that I tried to do something very bad last Friday night at the campout. But what you may not know is that I couldn't go through with it. At the last moment I got really scared. When I got back to my tent, I had to tell Darcelle about it. She didn't chew me out; she treated me like a real sister. She prayed for me, and when Liz came over to see what was going on, we prayed some more." Amber paused to wipe a small tear away from the corner of each eye.

"Ever since Duane and Liz came to our group, they've been telling us about how much God loves us and wants a relationship with us," Amber said. "Last Saturday morning at about 2:00 A.M. their message finally got through to me. With the help and prayers of Darcelle and Liz, I made a new commitment to trust Christ with my life and needs. For the first time, I think I'm beginning to understand God's love for me."

Somewhere inside him, Will felt his doors blow off. He stared at Amber with his mouth hanging open. In all the years he'd known her she'd never been so open about God in her life.

Just as Amber concluded her comments and sat down, there was a soft knock at the door, and Liz answered it.

"Here are our next two speakers, just in time," Duane said as the new guests entered. When Will turned to see who it was, he felt a half dozen more doors blow off inside him. "You all remember Reggie and Krystal from the campout,"

Duane continued. "They have some great news we want you to hear." Will's jaw hung slack.

Reggie was the first to speak.

"My main reason for going on the campout," he said, "was to be with Tony and Krystal. As you probably know, we did some things at the lake we shouldn't have. But I was also listening to what Duane was saying at the campfire, especially the story about the judge. I've always heard the bad-news side of religion—that unless I changed my ways I'd go to hell. Nobody ever told me the good news—that Jesus loved me enough to die for me so I wouldn't have to go to hell.

"A couple days after the campout, Duane called and asked if I wanted to get a burger with him—his treat. I was afraid he was going to rough me up about the beer and stuff, but I couldn't turn down a free meal." Everybody laughed.

"He just started telling me more about the fact that God loves me, Jesus died for me, and I can have a relationship with him based on love, not fear. It was so simple, so beautiful, so clear. That night at the golden arches I gave my life to Christ."

A burst of applause erupted. Buster, Darcelle, and Amber started it, but almost everybody joined in, including Will, who felt the inner campfire sensation again. A few kids even jumped up to hug Reggie or shake his hand.

Then Krystal told her story, explaining that Liz had met with her the same night and helped her trust Christ. Krystal also received a hero's salute.

After Reggie and Krystal sat down, Duane asked, "How many of you remember receiving an invitation to be part of a new prayer team for our group?" Almost everyone raised a hand, including Will, who had decided not to join the prayer team when he found out there would be no refreshments. "Well, a few of us have been meeting every week to pray for our youth group. Tonight you have seen what God can do when kids pray."

The prayer team had been praying that each member of the group would personally understand God's love and forgiveness, Duane said. He felt that Amber, Reggie, and Krystal were just the beginning of the answer to that prayer. As he talked, Will felt as if he was being left out in the cold. Something inside urged him to move closer to the warm, inviting flames.

"There may be some of you here tonight who are like Amber," Duane continued. Will swallowed hard. He had already made the comparison while she was speaking. "You've been playing the role of a nice little Christian kid, but you've been feeling frustrated and guilty. You probably haven't discovered how much God loves you and cares about you. We've been praying for you too. Wouldn't you like to see what a difference God can make in your life when you give Him control?"

Before Duane closed the meeting in prayer, he shared a verse that met a big need in Will's life. He read 1 John 1:9: "If we confess our sins, he is faithful and just and will forgive us our sins and purify us from all unrighteousness." It seemed so simple.

Why haven't I seen this before? Will wondered.

"You may know Christ personally," Duane explained, "but you may be carrying a load of guilt because of the way you've blown it as a Christian. What you don't know is that God still loves you unconditionally—no strings attached—and has already forgiven you. You just need to personally accept His forgiveness."

Duane asked those who wanted to turn control of their lives over to Christ to repeat a simple prayer after him—silently. Will's lips were tightly sealed, but his heart pronounced every word carefully: *Lord Jesus, thank You for loving me unconditionally, even when I blow it. I confess that I've been living my own life. Thank You for assuring me in 1 John 1:9 that my sin has been forgiven. Now, Lord, be my leader. Please give me Your power to follow and obey You. Amen.* The campfire within him suddenly erupted into a bonfire.

The Inside Story:
A New Start

Where are you in your relationship with God? Do you consciously give Christ the leadership of your life day after day? If so, even though things may not always be as you would like, you're finding a growing sense of satisfaction in your life. God's Word is really breaking through to help you grow in your faith and your relationship with God.

Perhaps that's not your experience, though. Oh, you believe in Christ and have trusted Him to forgive your sin. But you find yourself calling the shots in your life based on what you think is best. You just can't seem to find the time or desire to be with God in His Word and in prayer, so you just aren't getting the direction you need for your life. You go it alone most of the time—until a really big problem hits. Then you pray like crazy!

Life can be a struggle when you're calling the shots. You don't have much power over temptation, and you probably get discouraged more than you care to admit. You lack Christian joy, your anxiety level rises pretty high at times, and peace and power in your life are in short supply.

But you may be saying, "Hey, none of this Christian stuff relates to me. I'm not even sure I have a personal relationship with God. To be honest, I haven't trusted Christ to forgive my sins and come into my life."

If this is you, then you probably feel a deep emptiness that you sense can only be filled by God Himself. You've been searching for something to fill the vacuum in your life, otherwise you probably wouldn't be reading this book. God may be tugging at your heart, and soon you're going to have to decide whether you will trust Him to forgive your sin and be your Savior and Lord.

So the question remains: Where are you right now? Are you walking with the Lord every day? Are you mostly going it alone? Or are you still on the outside because you have never trusted Christ to be your Savior and Lord?

Once you decide just where you are in your relationship with God, you must answer another very important, very personal question: Where do you want to be? Silly question, right? Right! Anyone who gives it some serious thought would choose to be tight with God—close, intimate. Why would you want to walk around with the hassle of guilt and worry, not knowing just where you stand with the God of the universe, the God who created you? Why wouldn't you want to experience God's love, forgiveness, and power every day?

THE CHOICE IS YOURS

The great news is that you can make a choice. No matter where you are now, you can choose to make Christ the center of your life just as Will, Amber, Reggie, and Krystal did. If that's your choice, pay close attention to the rest of this chapter.

If you have never trusted Christ to forgive your sin and come into your life, you have a critical decision to make. Yes, you can know God personally. He is eager to establish a relationship with you, and He has made all the arrangements. He is patiently waiting for you to respond to His invitation. Please turn now to the Appendix of this book and carefully read the section, "Would You Like to Know God Personally?"

If you have trusted Christ in the past to forgive your sin, but you have been living a half-hearted, bogged-down Christian life, here are some practical steps to get you back on the right track.

1. Remember that God loves you unconditionally. You are His special child. He paid a high price—the death of His one and only Son, Jesus Christ—to reclaim you as His child. Your forgiveness was expensive, but God paid the price willingly (Romans 5:8).

Now, as a Christian, when you are disobedient, you grieve God (Ephesians 4:29–32). But His love for you never changes. He may discipline you to draw you near to Him (Hebrews 12:5–12), but His love stays consistent and perfect.

The problem is your sin, which is expressed in your attitudes and actions. The logical question, then, is, "How can I experience God's love and forgiveness when I sin?"

2. Confess your sin. Even though you are a Christian, you can still be hassled by what the Bible calls your sinful nature (Romans 7:20–25). And as you allow your sinful nature to have dominance in your life instead of God, the result is disobedience on your part—and a lot of unhappiness.

But God has provided a solution for your occasional lack of faith and disobedience as His child. According to God's Word, the solution begins with confession (1 John 1:9). To confess means to agree with God that your disobedience and lack of faith is sin. God is well aware of your attitudes and actions. But He is waiting for you to agree with Him. By doing so, you humble yourself before God and experience God's grace and power (1 Peter 5:5–6).

3. Claim God's forgiveness. Confession does not mean you receive more of God's forgiveness. Christ has already forgiven you once and for all through His death on the cross (Hebrews 10:12–14; 1 Peter 3:18). You can't get more forgiveness. Rather, you must claim and accept the forgiveness that is already yours.

In claiming God's forgiveness you accept by faith what God has said to you in His Word. As you do, He will help you experience the incredible truth of your forgiveness in your life. It's like discovering a treasure that was always yours because it was buried in your own backyard. You are loved and forgiven by God. Claim it and enjoy it!

4. Turn to God and trust Him. A commitment to Christ is really a willful decision to trust and obey Him. It's like saying to God, "I've made a decision to trust You. Accepting Your love for me and obeying You is the best way I can demonstrate my gratitude and love to You."

When you turn to God and trust Him, you change your attitudes and actions. You make a decision to turn to God instead of continuing to think or do those things that have caused you to drift in your relationship with Christ.

"Hey, it's tough to change my attitudes and actions!" you may say. On your own, it's not only tough, it's impossible! That's why you must trust God. By trusting in Him you are depending on His power and strength to live the Christian life (2 Timothy 2:22).

It's important to remember, too, that turning to Him and trusting Him are not things you do once and then put behind you. You must *live* the same way you were *saved.* Just as you can't save yourself from your sins, you cannot *live* the Christian life in your own strength. Galatians 2:20 speaks of the old nature being put to death and Christ now living through you. Yield to Him every day, constantly, and allow Him to live His life in you.

The first letters of *agree* with God, *claim* His forgiveness, and *turn* to Him spell *act.* Whenever you find sin in your life, confession is the willful, purposeful act that allows you to resume a close, intimate relationship with God.

Take a sheet of paper right now and complete this "act" in writing. List all the ways you can think of by which you have been living independent from God. As you write, agree with God that these attitudes and behaviors are wrong. Claim God's forgiveness by writing the reference "1 John 1:9" across your list in large, bold characters. Then destroy the sheet, signifying that you have confessed your sins and claimed God's forgiveness.

As important as it is, making the willful, conscious decision to put Christ at the center of your life is just the beginning. You need to establish a winning lifestyle that reflects your decision, even when you face opposition from below. Will, Amber, Reggie, Krystal, and their friends are about to find out all about it.

4

Blue-White Terror

It had not been a good week for Demon Ratsbane. After igniting the argument between Tony Ortiz and Duane Cunningham, he had been constantly transmitting impulses to prevent Duane's campfire talks about the Enemy's love from taking root in Will, Jason, Joy, and the others. But in all his activity, Ratsbane had overlooked two kids from the campout he hadn't been very concerned about. A squawk from Stygios triggered a horrifying flurry of activities for the new PIT operator.

On one monitor, Liz Cunningham sat in the living room of their apartment next to a girl with streaky, bleach-blonde hair. On another monitor, Duane and a tall, husky boy sat across from each other in a booth at a McDonald's. Liz and Duane were assuring Krystal and Reggie respectively that the Enemy loves them and wants to forgive their sin and fill their lives with Himself. The couple were listening intently, and the conduits above Ratsbane started to shudder noisily.

Buoyed by his recent success, Ratsbane confidently launched a blinding barrage of impulses in both directions. He beat the ME button so furiously that it began to smoke.

"Lies, lies, lies!" he bellowed at the two young people. "The Enemy doesn't love you. He just wants to rip off your freedom and your fun! Think of yourselves." But the increasing power Ratsbane poured into his transmissions only caused the conduits to pop, crackle, and spark more.

That's when Ratsbane encountered his first brigadiers. Liz and Krystal had just joined hands and bowed their heads. Ratsbane was firing impulses frantically at the two women when a blue-white flash appeared on the screen between them. In a fraction of a second the flash congealed into a large, muscular figure dressed in a sparkling blue-and-white uniform. The figure began to circle Krystal in a simple dance. Faster and faster he twirled around the girl as she prayed some words Liz had suggested. Then Ratsbane saw another blue-white form appear on the other monitor, circling Reggie.

"By all that's heinous, what are those?" Ratsbane screeched, his steely composure beginning to crack.

"Brigadiers!" Marplot whined above the noise as he turned from his own duties to help the new recruit. "They're members of the Enemy's angelic light brigade, invisible to humans. They can shatter the blindness of the captives. The brigadiers are too strong for the PIT, Ratsbane. Back off on the power or you'll blow the main circuits."

But Ratsbane, angered and terrified by what he saw on the monitors, let out a hideous yowl and leaped onto the console, working ferociously at the keyboards and controls. The PIT howled and moaned as the monitors flashed and the conduits flooded with impulses.

"You can't beat them, Ratsbane!" cried Marplot in terror. "Cut your power and save the PIT! Their blindness is dissolving in the awful light. You've lost them!"

"Never!" Ratsbane insisted. He continued to jump and pound on the controls. Monitors flickered with scrambled symbols and images. Conduits began to shatter, and some of the buttons and dials began to explode from the panel like popcorn.

But the brigadiers were unaffected. Instead, they danced so rapidly around the two teenagers that all Ratsbane could see was a brilliant cylinder of blue-white light surrounding each of them. Marplot and Stygios scrambled for cover in sheer panic before the cylinders severed the PIT lines and the impulses backed up into the conduits. But they were too late. The brigadier encircling Krystal quickly burned through her PIT lines, and seconds later the boy was also free.

Two horrendous explosions rocked the PIT cave. Chunks of polished stone from shattered conduits and panels ricocheted around the walls like bullets. Hundreds of exposed cables sizzled and popped. Sparks and flame shot from ceiling to floor and back again. A couple of nearby maintenance runts were vaporized into puffs of yellow-green smoke. Minutes later Ratsbane, Marplot, and Stygios could be heard moaning under the smoldering rubble.

That was Wednesday. On Friday night it happened again. The three demons had barely recovered from the first attack and finished some basic repairs on the PIT when the video party at the Cunninghams' turned into a mini-revival. Frenzied with anger and fear, Ratsbane again launched all the firepower he could muster from the clattering, backfiring PIT in his attempt to keep Will, Jason, and Joy from committing themselves to be radicals for the Enemy. But his salvos were easily deflected by a platoon of brigadiers who stood guard around Duane and Liz's living room. For the second time in a week, the PIT cave resembled the rubble-strewn target of a squadron of stealth bombers.

It took hours for Ratsbane, Marplot, and Stygios to separate themselves from the debris again and begin to assess the damage to the cave. The PIT was still operational, but just barely. Huge sections of the console had been blown away and several monitors had been shattered by chunks of flying stone. A couple dozen conduits had exploded down to jagged stumps, and the severed cables drooped from them like dead flowers in a vase.

The PIT operators themselves wore marks of the battle. Marplot suffered a shattered hoof and several broken teeth.

Stygios' pelican beak was bent several degrees to one side. One of Ratsbane's antennae was missing, and he'd developed a severe tic in one of his huge eyes from the trauma he had suffered.

Ratsbane's insides churned like a cauldron of boiling acid as he watched a platoon of runts swarm into the cave and begin to piece the PIT back together. He had never known such hatred and such terror in all the eons of his existence. He loathed the Enemy, the brigadiers, and the radicals for spoiling his debut in Subsector 477, and he bitterly vowed his revenge. But he was secretly terrified at the Enemy's power.

Can the brigadiers really sever PIT lines at will? he thought. *Can the rebels advance the Enemy's rebellion virtually unopposed?*

He glanced around suspiciously. He knew that his thoughts had leapt into forbidden areas. He knew that his clashing emotions of rage and terror represented the great "Catch-22" for every demon in hell—including Satan himself. Being one in nature with Satan, Ratsbane and his kind were bitterly opposed to the Enemy and everyone who belonged to Him. But since they were inferior in power to their Enemy, the brigadiers and the Spirit-filled rebels, the creatures of the underworld faced ultimate defeat no matter how many momentary victories they achieved.

Ratsbane was getting his first taste of the eternal double bind. His loathing for the Enemy urged him to continue opposing Him, but the prospect of imminent defeat terrified him. He hadn't quite figured it out, but his hateful opposition would continue to lead to terrifying defeat, which would spur him to even angrier opposition followed by even more terrifying defeat. This vicious, no-win cycle is what made life hell for mutants like Ratsbane.

Marplot, who was slumped next to Ratsbane against the cave wall, seemed to read his thoughts. "Come with me to the keyboard."

Marplot pieced together enough circuitry to get several monitors working. On each one he pulled up a live shot of the kids who had attended the video party and were now all sleeping in their beds. Ratsbane studied them with one eye twitching wildly in disdain.

"You can't tell by looking at them now, but each one of them is tapped into a power source that is capable of reducing every PIT in hell to a pile of gravel," Marplot said, trembling with the same rage and terror Ratsbane felt.

"But there are no power lines attached to them," Ratsbane argued weakly.

"They don't need power lines," Marplot snapped. "Their power source is actually within them: the Enemy's Spirit. And as long as His Spirit fills them they are virtually unstoppable. When they are on the march, the Enemy is pleased to deploy His brigadiers in their aid. Unless you can find a way to smother the little revival that has ignited in these rebels, Subsector 477 is doomed."

"So what can I do to disarm the rebels and snuff them out?" Ratsbane tried to pose his question in a hateful, vindictive tone, but it came out sounding more like a whimper.

"Disrupt the continuity of the power source within them. Their strength lies in their daily, personal relationship with the Enemy—that is their PowerLink. Get them thinking about religion instead: following rules, attending meetings, trying to earn the Enemy's approval. They get a lot of strength from reading their Book. Distract them from it. They help each other remain strong when they hang out together. Drive them apart. And most of all, keep them from pray—"

Marplot was suddenly tongue-tied and seized with fear. Ratsbane saw that the big demon was looking past him to the cave entrance. He turned to see a huge python with a swan's head slithering toward them.

The first two weeks of the semester went well for Will. He was ahead on most of his assignments at school, and he'd finally simulated a landing at LA International airport on his Mac after dunking his first four 747s in the Pacific Ocean.

Somehow he expected that the kids who were at the video party would act differently toward each other at school. He did notice that Amber stayed as far away from Tony as possible, which wasn't difficult since he always had two or three other girls around him anyway. And Reggie and Krystal certainly seemed different around the campus. But the youth group as a whole still acted like strangers. *That's weird,* Will thought, *considering that we shared such a great time together at the Cunninghams' that night.*

Will hadn't told anyone about his decision to give the controls of his life to Christ, not even Amber. He didn't want Amber to think he was copying her, or worse yet, suspect that he still had a crush on her, which he did. But he also hadn't confessed his decision because he was confused about just what he had committed himself *to.* He had felt great that night—the glowing inner fire and everything. And he was pretty sure he did the right thing, the thing God wanted him to do. But since that night his inner glow had all but fizzled out. He didn't think or feel any different than before. He had no burning urge to read the Bible and pray every day like Darcelle. And he still scared himself with occasional steamy thoughts, and Amber was often in the middle of them.

Will had hoped he would be a different person after that night at the Cunninghams', but he wasn't—at least as far as he could tell. And he wasn't sure what kind of difference he should look for anyway. So he decided to take a big step. Darcelle had invited him to the first meeting of the prayer team since the campout, and he decided to go. He might not get any refreshments, but he hoped he'd get unconfused about what had happened to him.

Will was not surprised to find Darcelle and Buster at the meeting Thursday night. He knew they were the heart of the prayer team. But he was a little surprised to see Amber, Reggie, and Krystal there, and he was very surprised at two of the faces looking up at him when he entered the living room: Jason Withers and Joy Akiyama. *Did they make a new commitment to Christ too?* Will wondered.

The way Duane started the meeting made Will very uncomfortable: "Our prayer group has grown since the last meeting. Let's go around the circle and everybody tell why you decided to come." Will didn't know how honest he wanted to be. After all the Sunday school attendance pins he had earned over the years, he didn't want to sound like a dweeb in the faith, even though he knew he was one.

Duane started on the side of the circle where the regular members were sitting, which gave Will time to think about what to say. Buster and Darcelle, who were bubbling about the increase in attendance, talked about wanting to see God's power continue to work in the group through prayer. *Oh, brother!* Will groaned inside. *Nice holy thought, but nobody would believe me if I said something like that—even me.*

Reggie's answer was completely different: "As you know, I'm kind of new at all this Christian stuff like praying and reading the Bible. I'm here because I thought you guys could give me some tips on being a Christian." Krystal agreed with Reggie. Their answers were a lot closer to what Will was feeling. But he still hated to admit that he needed a course in bonehead Christianity when everybody knew he'd been in the system most of his life.

Amber made things a little easier.

"I believe in prayer, but I'm here mainly because I need to be with other Christians. I've changed a lot of my priorities in the past couple of weeks, but I kind of feel like a loner at school. I'm afraid if I don't get some support from you guys I'm not going to make it."

Jason shocked Will with his honesty and seriousness.

"At the meeting two weeks ago, I confessed some things to God and recommitted my life to Christ during that silent prayer. I'm here because I want to learn how to grow in my walk with God and learn how to pray for our group." Jason paused, then concluded as only Jason could: "And I'm also here because I was hoping there was some ice cream left over from the video party."

"All right!" Will added, and the group enjoyed a good laugh.

Quiet little Joy Akiyama admitted that Duane's talk two weeks earlier had opened her eyes to God's love and forgiveness. She had also prayed the silent prayer. She said she came to tonight's meeting so she could learn more about a loving relationship with God.

Then it was Will's turn. He looked around the circle and suddenly felt real good about being with them. He wasn't very close to any of them, but he was closer to these kids—and to Duane and Liz—than to anyone else he knew. He felt that he could be totally honest with them or totally phony and they wouldn't reject him. He opted for honesty.

"I wasn't sure why I decided to come tonight. But after hearing all of you, I think I know. I also prayed with Duane at the video party, but since then I've been wondering what it means to open my life to God. I need to know more about Him. I mean, how does He really give us the power we need? Like Amber, I need support, and like Jason, I still have a lot to learn. It sounds like being together might be the best thing for all of us." Several heads nodded.

After a silent, thoughtful moment, Duane spoke. "I really appreciate your honesty in sharing tonight. What you have said confirms in my heart the next thing God wants us to learn as individuals and as a group. Not only do we need to continue to pray for each other, but we need to learn just how God plans to work in us by His Spirit. And we need to start discovering what it means to be Christ's disciples. I suggest that we begin studying and praying together regularly and help each other grow in our walk with God. What do you think?"

The response was unanimous. After a lively discussion, they all joined hands and prayed for each other. Before the meeting was over, the group agreed to meet every Thursday night.

As he walked home, Will suddenly remembered the clumsy, angry prayer he had fired off to God shortly after he discovered Amber in the woods with Reggie, Krystal, and Tony: You'd better do something about Tony Ortiz, God.

"Strange to think of that now," Will mumbled. "What does that prayer have to do with what happened tonight?"

The Inside Story: A Winning Lifestyle

What do you think of when you hear the word *disciple?* Many of us imagine the original twelve disciples wandering all over Palestine with Jesus, then scampering into the darkness like cowards when He was crucified. But we also remember that most of them were in the right place when the Holy Spirit was poured out nearly two months later. It is rather interesting that these disciples spent the rest of their lives serving Christ, most of them becoming martyrs in the process. Now that's commitment! If you're thinking that the Holy Spirit must make a difference in people's lives, you're right.

Do you ever think of yourself as a disciple? "Not me," you may answer. "I'm not into facial hair, and bathrobes are really out of style this year. Besides, I can't drop out of school to follow Christ full time. And even if I could, I'm not sure martyrdom agrees with me."

Whether you think of yourself as a disciple or not, if you have chosen to follow Christ, you are one. If you have entered into a personal relationship with Jesus, you have already met the first requirement for discipleship. You are a modern-day disciple, part of God's army. And the way God wants to work in and through you is very similar to how He has been using His other disciples over the last two thousand years.

However, there is a lot to learn about being a disciple. And discovering just how God works in you by His Spirit is the first lesson.

TAPPING INTO YOUR POWER SOURCE

We discussed earlier that living the Christian life isn't hard, it's impossible. If fact, there's only one Person who has ever lived a perfect Christian life, and that was Jesus Christ Himself.

Maybe that's why we're called Christians. The word Christian actually means "Christ in you." You can only live the Christian life by allowing Christ to take up residence in your life and develop His qualities through you. That's supernatural, but then that's what Christianity and being a disciple is all about.

Like Will, Amber, Jason, and the rest of the group, we have a lot to learn about Christ's life within us. The Bible actually calls it the Spirit-filled life. Let's take a look at this person who is so vital to our walk with God, the Holy Spirit.

The Bible teaches us that the Holy Spirit is God's Spirit. This means that the Holy Spirit is not a thing or a phantom but a living person with personality and feelings. The Holy Spirit is one of the members of the Trinity: God the Father, God the Son (Jesus Christ), and God the Holy Spirit.

When you became a Christian, God's Spirit actually entered your life (Romans 8:9; 1 Corinthians 3:16). Because the Holy Spirit is God, He is omnipresent. That means He can be everywhere at once. He can live in you and in other Christians around the world at the same time.

It is through the Holy Spirit that God does His work in our lives. For example, the Holy Spirit enables us to understand the Bible (John 14:26). He gives us courage and the words we need to share Christ with others (Acts 1:8). And He develops in us the qualities that make us winners in our relationship with God and others. These qualities are called the fruit of the Spirit: love, joy, peace, patience, kindness, goodness, faithfulness, gentleness, and self-control (Galatians 5:22–23).

Here's another great thing the Holy Spirit does. As illustrated in the story about Will and his group and Ratsbane and his fellow demons, there is a war going on over you. But when you trusted Christ, the Holy Spirit actually claimed and sealed you for God (Ephesians 4:30; 2 Corinthians 1:21–22). You belong to God now, and Satan has lost you forever.

But while Satan no longer owns you, he doesn't stop trying to neutralize you as a Christian. He wants your faith to diminish to the point that you are no longer effective for God (Ephesians 6:1–12).

How should you deal with Satan's clever tactics to neutralize you? The answer is in Paul's prayer for the young Ephesian Christians. He prayed that God would strengthen each of them "with power through his Spirit in your inner being" (Ephesians 3:16). The point is simple but radically profound. It is only by God's Spirit that you have the strength to live your Christian life.

PRINCIPLES FOR POWER

You must allow the Holy Spirit to fill you and take charge of your life. How do you do that? Here are three simple principles that will help you be filled by and walk in the power of God's Holy Spirit—the key to your PowerLink!

1. Confess your sin (1 John 1:9). Earlier we talked about the importance of confession in your walk with God. The principles are just as applicable to being a Spirit-filled Christian. The Holy Spirit cannot fill and lead you when you choose to live independent from God. That's why people like Will,

Amber, Jason, and Joy lived such unfulfilled lives even as Christians.

Whenever you realize that you have been disobedient to God and are in control of your life, you must agree that your independence is wrong. By faith, claim God's love and the forgiveness for sin He has promised you. Remember: You are completely forgiven because Christ paid the ultimate price for your sin through His death.

When you confess, you are humbling yourself before God and saying, "I'm wrong and You are right. Thank You for continuing to love and forgive me." When you express this humble attitude, God makes real in your experience what He has already done for you through the death of His Son Jesus. God sure is good!

2. Trust God to fill you and lead you by His Spirit. Will's inner flame grew to bonfire proportions that evening at Duane's house as he sensed God's love and forgiveness. Talk about refreshing! Will probably didn't even realize how little he knew about God's love for him. At the moment Will prayed his prayer of commitment, God caused him to experience the reality of His love and forgiveness deep inside.

But for Will and a lot of Christians, knowing God's love and forgiveness and acting on them every day can be two different things. God calls us to respond to His love by allowing Him to be Lord of our lives and fill us with His Spirit. Being filled with the Spirit means that He is directing our lives and giving us His power to resist temptation, gain courage, make right choices, and deal with everything that happens in our lives each day.

What must you do to be filled with the Holy Spirit?

First, present every area of your life to God (Romans 12:1–2). Ask God to help you identify everything in your life—activities, friends, desires, etc.—and tell Him you want Him to be your leader in each area.

Second, ask the Holy Spirit to fill you. God commands us to be filled with the Holy Spirit (Ephesians 5:18). Asking to be filled is a clear step of obedience.

Third, believe that He fills you when you ask Him to. The Holy Spirit is a free gift to be received. As you pray and express your request to be filled, God promises to answer (1 John 5:14–15).

Is it God's will for you to be filled with His Spirit? Yes. Will He fill you if you ask Him to? You can count on it! The following is a suggested prayer for expressing your desire to be filled with the Holy Spirit: "Dear Father, I need You. I acknowledge that I have been directing my life and that, as a result, I have sinned against You. I thank You that You have forgiven my sins through Christ's death on the cross for me. I now invite Christ to again take His place on the throne of my life. Fill me with the Holy Spirit as you commanded me to be filled, and as You promised in Your Word that You would do if I asked in faith. I now thank You for directing my life and for filling me with the Holy Spirit."

Do you feel differently when you are filled with God's Spirit? Not necessarily. Being filled with the Spirit is not so much a matter of feeling as it is a matter of fact. God fills us because He promises in His Word to do so. That's fact! Feelings come and go. The greatest evidence of God's control in your life is the peace, power, and fruit of the Spirit you will experience.

3. Keep walking in the Spirit. Just because you trust God to fill you with His Spirit doesn't mean that you will never blow it through lack of faith or disobedience. No one is perfect. And besides, you have to contend with a sinful world around you and the devil himself. But you can live more consistently day after day if you apply these simple principles.

First, when you blow it, confess your sin quickly and turn back to God. Ask Him to fill you again with His Spirit and trust Him to do so. Keep short accounts with God. The longer you put off dealing with sin in your life, the more distant you become in your walk with God. And when you sense a distance between you and God, who moved? You did! Move back right away.

Second, build your faith through your study of God's Word and through prayer (Romans 10:17). Your involvement in these disciplines is vital to your faith. They cleanse and transform your mind and disarm Satan's tactics. Set aside regular time to involve yourself in Bible study and prayer.

Third, be prepared for spiritual conflict against the world (1 John 2:15–17), the flesh (Galatians 5:16–21), and Satan (1 Peter 5:8–9). Respond to the conflict by relying on God's Spirit working in you and through you.

Disciples are people who are learning to allow Christ to live His life through them. Discipleship requires faith and humility, but the rewards are incredible. The Spirit-filled life of disciples are not an elective; it's required. Why? Because discipleship is a prerequisite for the mission to which God has called each of us. As they begin to take steps of faith as Christ's disciples, Will McConnell and his friends will come face to face with this mission.

5

The Bag Lady's Revenge

Will rummaged through his closet murmuring to himself. He hadn't been able to come up with an idea for a costume, and he had to leave for the Cunninghams' in ten minutes. He didn't have an idea mainly because he didn't want to have an idea. He thought wearing a costume to the prayer team meeting was dumb even if it did happen to fall on Halloween night. But he'd been outvoted nine to one; everybody else wanted to dress in costume.

Will was also a little out of sorts because Jason had refused to help him find a costume. Will knew that Jason would wear something wild and crazy to the meeting. In fact, Jason would come to school in costume every day if he could. He had a big trunk in his closet jammed full of masks, wigs, hats, crazy clothes, and props he'd found in thrift stores. He would often show up at a prayer team meeting or fun night wearing an old pith helmet or a pair of sunglasses with one lens knocked out. But when Will had asked if he could borrow something from Jason's trunk, Jason had answered, "Nobody gets into my trunk, not even my best friend."

Jason even said he would meet Will at the Cunninghams' instead of walking over with him as he usually did. "Some best friend, leaving me out in the cold on Halloween night," Will harrumphed.

At the bottom of a pile of junk in the corner of his closet Will found the Pirates jersey and batting helmet his father had sent him for Christmas two years ago. Being more of a Dodgers fan, Will had stashed them with other unused gifts from distant relatives. He hoped to hold his own gigantic yard sale some day. *This will have to do,* he thought as he donned the jersey and helmet, then grabbed his Bible and headed for the door.

Then he remembered something he was trying to teach himself not to forget. He went to the answering machine, punched the memo button and recorded his message: "Welcome home, Mom. Hope your meetings in Phoenix went okay. I'm at the Cunninghams' for our regular Thursday night meeting. See you when I get home about 10:00. I love you."

Will appreciated and respected his mother, but he had never felt very close to her. As the marketing director for a large electronics firm, Dorina McConnell had provided well for her only child in the ten years since Will's father left. After all, Will didn't know too many sophomores who had their own Mac, laser printer, and all the software they could use.

But Dorina was so wrapped up in providing a comfortable life for them that she rarely had much time for Will. They rode to church together on Sunday mornings when she was in town, and she always took him out to eat afterward. But her evenings and weekends were often consumed with business activities, leaving Will home alone with his Mac. Will knew she had his best interests at heart, but her emotional absence seemed almost as painful to him as his father's physical absence.

"Your relationship with your family is second only to your relationship with Christ," Will remembered Duane teaching on Thursday nights. "God has placed you in your parents' home to help you develop as His disciple, whether they're perfect or not. If you aren't developing a loving relationship at home, you won't get very far in your relationship with Christ." Will walked out the door hoping his mom would feel his love when she got home and heard the message.

As he approached the Cunninghams' apartment, Will noticed a commotion on the sidewalk under the lamppost. A gang of older trick-or-treaters were harassing and taunting a stoop-shouldered, heavyset bag lady pushing a rickety shopping cart piled high with bulging Hefty bags. The woman wore a long, tattered coat, and a woolen muffler covered most of her head and face. Occasionally one of the kids would reach out and poke her as if on a dare. The woman waved her arm at them, trying to drive them away, but that only encouraged them.

As Will drew closer, the woman's plaintive eyes peeked out at him from her muffler, begging for his aid. He stood there a few seconds, dumbfounded, not knowing what to do.

Suddenly the woman took matters into her own hands. In one swift motion she reached into her cart, pulled out a long-handled ax and swept it high above her head. She let out such a bloodcurdling scream that half the kids fell over from fright. The woman seemed intent on plunging the ax into the slowest of the terrified kids scrambling to escape. So Will let out a scream of his own. "Stop, ma'am! Don't do it!" He was rushing toward the woman to grab the ax when she abruptly turned on him. Glancing at the dull gray blade poised above him, Will felt every ounce of blood desert his head. *I wonder if Amber will cry at my funeral,* he thought as his knees began to buckle.

That's when the woman's muffler fell off. "Trick or treat, Will," Jason said, a mischievous grin lighting up his heavily made-up bag-lady face. Will knew in an instant he'd been had again by the greatest prankster alive. Jason dropped the head of the plastic toy ax harmlessly on Will's baseball helmet. Then they both fell to the grass in a laughing fit.

Jason's antics and Will's reaction were the talk of the group as they scarfed down bowls of chili and cups of cider served by Liz. And Will enjoyed every minute of it. The prayer team had really started to blend together as a group of friends since they started meeting six weeks ago. Will no longer felt laughed at by them. He knew they were too close for that.

After dinner Duane led the group through a meeting that had become standard operating procedure for them since they committed to meet together. First, everybody would share what they had learned in their daily, personal quiet times with God through the week. Then Duane or Liz would give a little talk; tonight it was Liz's turn. Finally, they divided up into small groups and prayed for each other as growing disciples of Christ.

Amber was first to speak during sharing time. She was dressed as a princess in her mom's old formal, heaps of gaudy jewelry, and a Burger King crown.

"I guess," she began, "God's been kinda making me . . ." She hesitated, searching for the right words. "Giving me a new appreciation, I guess, for my parents' strictness. I mean, I still wish they'd give me more freedom sometimes, but I have to admit they've also kept me from making some pretty big mistakes."

Will knew exactly what she was talking about.

Both Reggie and Krystal, who came dressed as Laurel and Hardy, had some questions about the new believer's Bible study Duane had given them to work through. Reggie talked about his struggle with turning away from some of his old habits. Krystal testified that she had been "clean" for over a month, thanks to Darcelle and her mother. Krystal had moved in with them to escape the negative influence of a father who was still dealing.

Even Joy Akiyama, the freckle-faced, oriental Raggedy Ann sitting across from Will, had come out of her shell somewhat during these sharing times. He was amazed at how much she had internalized about Christ and the Bible during her years as a nominal Christian. Many of her quietly stated insights about being Christ's disciple had caused him to change his own thinking in some areas. And even though Will didn't know the details, Darcelle had told him that Joy was finally making some headway in dealing with her parents.

Jason talked about how God was leading him to spend more time in his Bible and less time in front of the television. Will knew more about Jason's problem than Jason admitted to the whole group. With Will's mom and Jason's parents out of the home so much, the two of them had spent a lot of time together since the prayer team became a discipleship group. Once, when sleeping over at Jason's, Will woke up in the middle of the night to find his friend in the family room watching an X-rated movie on the cable. Will watched for a minute in shocked amazement. He found it hard to turn away from the horrible action on the screen. But finally, with a quick turn, he went back to bed without saying a word to Jason.

It took Will a couple of days of prayer to work up the nerve to confront Jason about his porn habit. Jason was angry and defensive at first, but then he admitted that he couldn't help watching the stuff when he was home alone. Jason cried; then the two of them prayed. Will committed himself to pray for Jason every day and to hold him accountable—all in strict confidence. They agreed that this new dimension to their friendship couldn't have happened six months earlier.

Will shared with the group how his relationship with his mother was improving. He mentioned the memo he had left her on the answering machine, and his friends lavished him with "attaboys" for doing so.

Will had not told the group much about his father. He knew some day he would explain why his father's last name was different than his, that his father and mother were never married, that he was an illegitimate child. It was something Will was ashamed of, something he had only told Jason two weeks ago—and nobody else. Somehow he knew a time would come when he would feel okay about telling the rest of his friends.

Then it was time for Liz's talk. "I was reading in Colossians during my devotions this week, and Colossians 1:13 really jumped out at me." Pages fluttered as the circle of disciples located Colossians in their Bibles. "As I read it and prayed about it, I realized that what God was telling me in this verse was something our group needs to hear. These last six weeks have been great as we have grown together as a group. But I think God wants us to lean even closer to Him and listen to His heartbeat. Would somebody please read Colossians 1:13 aloud?"

Darcelle cleared her throat. "For he has rescued us from the dominion of darkness and brought us into the kingdom of the Son he loves."

Liz continued. "Some of us have been Christians for a long time, while kids like Reggie and Krystal have only been believers a few weeks. But when I read this verse God seemed to be reminding me that His rescue job at Eisenhower High School isn't over. There are still lots of kids who are chained in the darkness. God loves those kids as much as He loves us. He wants to rescue them too. Rescuing people from the darkness is God's heartbeat."

Will had heard everything Liz was saying before, from some youth retreats he had attended. He'd heard so much about the lost and the importance of evangelism that Liz's words about God's heartbeat seemed to bounce off him. Even during small group prayer, Will found his mind wandering while Jason, Reggie, Buster, and Duane asked God to show the group how to get in tune with His heartbeat.

But exactly twenty-four hours later Liz's words stopped bouncing and scored a direct hit on Will McConnell. It was during the fourth quarter. The Eisenhower Generals, led by Tony Ortiz's powerful running, were annihilating their cross-town rivals, Westcastle Union, 48–6. And Tony was within sixteen yards of setting a school record for yardage.

Will was squashed in between Jason and Buster Todd in the student section which had been on its feet and yelling itself hoarse since the opening kickoff. "Look at that rhino run!" Jason cheered, waving his pith helmet aloft. Tony had just followed a block by guard Reggie Spencer through a hole in the line and rambled for eight more yards. The entire student section broke into a deafening *stomp-stomp-clap, stomp-stomp-clap* that rocked the old wooden stadium. Will could see Amber down on the track, arms flying and legs prancing as she stepped out the cheers.

The Generals ran the play again. Reggie pulled out of his guard position on the left, swept to the right, cut upfield, and sent the linebacker sprawling with a crushing block. Tony, following closely, leaped over the linebacker, cut sharply inside to elude the cornerback, and sprinted untouched into the end zone.

The team swamped Tony at the goal line. Then as the rest of the team trotted to the sidelines, two players stayed in the end zone a few seconds longer. Reggie Spencer was bowed on one knee, and Will knew he was thanking God for his ability. Standing next to Reggie, waving his helmet triumphantly and drinking in the thunderous applause of the crowd, was Tony.

Will suddenly saw the contrast as never before. There was Reggie, a new believer, rescued from the darkness of a life without Christ. Reggie had trusted Christ and it even showed on the football field. And there was Tony, the proud, self-centered hero, chained in a dungeon away from the God who loves him and died for him. His reputation around school for wild living matched his performance that night at the campout. As much as he hated what Tony had done to Amber, Will knew that he was desperately in need of being rescued.

As Reggie and Tony ran off the field Will's weeks-old prayer leaped into his conscious mind, and he prayed it again: *You'd better do something about Tony, God.* As he stared at Tony, it seemed to Will that the stadium was empty and silent except for him in the stands and Tony on the field. Everything that Will had ever heard about evangelism suddenly crystallized into words that seemed to blare at him from an inner loudspeaker: "I'm doing my part, Will. It's time for you to do something about Tony."

The Inside Story: Listening to God's Heartbeat

They often look the same to us too, don't they? Believers and unbelievers on the football team all wear the same uniform. Believers and unbelievers sitting around you in algebra, chem lab, band, and German class just look like kids trying to get a decent grade and fit in with the crowd: no halos circling over the Christians, no horns on the heads of the non-Christians.

But there is a difference—a critical, eternal difference. As Liz suggested in her talk, unbelievers are imprisoned in the darkness, separated from God and eternal life. They follow the ways of this world. They live under the rulership of Satan. They are chained to their sinful nature and follow its desires and thoughts (Ephesians 2:1–3). But we who have trusted Christ are in the kingdom of light (1 John 1:5–7). God in His great love has rescued us from the darkness and brought us into the eternal kingdom of His Son, Jesus Christ (Colossians 1:13).

Like Will, many of us have heard about this difference so often for so long that the reality of it just bounces off us. We're easily lulled into complacency because the difference isn't as obvious to us as the similarities.

GOD'S HEART BEATS FOR THOSE IN DARKNESS

God hasn't forgotten about the difference. He is acutely aware that untold millions of people—including hundreds and possibly thousands in your school and community—still live in the darkness without Christ. He is incredibly concerned for each one—*so* concerned, in fact, that He took the ultimate step for every student, mom, and dad. He became a man and gave His life (Romans 5:8).

When someone is lost, it's serious business to God. He's not willing that any should perish (2 Peter 3:9). As Liz said, God's rescue operation is not over.

The apostle Paul picked up on the broad scope of God's intended rescue effort. He wrote: "Though I am free and belong to no man, I make myself a slave to everyone, to win as many as possible. . . . I have become all things to all men so that by all possible means I might save some" (1 Corinthians 9:19, 22). Paul was close enough to God to hear His heartbeat: Rescue the lost. And Paul committed his life to the task.

THE RESCUED BECOME THE RESCUERS

The most important news for us about God's rescue effort is that He allows us the privilege of being involved in it. He could do it by Himself if He wanted. But He has appointed the rescued (if you have trusted Christ, that's *you*) to work with Him as rescuers.

Jesus compared God's rescue mission to a grain harvest. He challenges us to pray that more harvesters will become available so that more of the lost can be "harvested" (Matthew 9:37–38). Paul refers to us as God's ambassadors who have been given the ministry of taking His message of salvation to others (2 Corinthians 5:18–20).

Are all those chained in darkness going to be rescued? No. Tragically, many have refused to be rescued in the past, and many others will refuse in the future. But there are many others who are just waiting for someone to tell them of God's unconditional love and that Christ has set them free. So, like Paul, we tell as many people as possible so that as many of them as possible may be rescued.

EVANGELISM: TELLING THE GOOD NEWS AND MAKING DISCIPLES

Our participation in God's rescue mission is called evangelism. Generally speaking, evangelism means communicating the good news of Jesus Christ to those who are lost and in darkness. More specifically, the Bible reveals three activities that must be included if our communication of the good news is to be called true evangelism.

1. Tell the facts (1 Corinthians 15:1–4). There's a sense in which the way you conduct yourself around non-Christians is a witness to them. If you're living by the Bible's guidelines, for example, you don't cheat on homework or exams, you aren't "boozing, using, or cruising for sex," and you're respectful toward parents and teachers.

That's wonderful, but it's not evangelism. The good news centers on what God has done to free your non-Christian friends from sin and introduce them to His love. At some point in your witness, you need to tell them that Jesus' death and resurrection has provided forgiveness for their sin and eternal life, and that they must turn and trust Christ to claim God's provision. You haven't really started to evangelize until you tell them the facts.

2. Call for a decision (2 Corinthians 5:11, 20). Imagine that you just discovered a potion that cures cancer. You are ecstatic because your best friend has cancer. You not only tell your friend about the potion, but you do everything in your power to persuade him to take it. The fact that a cure exists is not enough. Your friend must take the potion, or your discovery will do him no good.

Similarly, you must do what you can to persuade your non-Christian friends to respond to God's provision for their rescue. Knowing the facts isn't enough. They must trust Christ personally or the good news is not good news for them.

Sharing the facts and persuading non-Christians to respond doesn't mean that you threaten or pester people until they can't stand to be around you. Rather, in reasoning with them and convincing them about the facts, you lovingly challenge them to change their minds about God and trust Christ. You haven't fully evangelized them until you give them an opportunity to make a decision.

3. Make disciples (Matthew 28:19–20). Jesus clearly revealed that the ultimate result of evangelism is a disciple. When Reggie and Krystal trusted Christ, Duane and Liz began to disciple the two new believers, realizing that they needed to be taught and encouraged if they were to grow up in the faith and become mature believers.

Introducing your non-Christian friends to Christ includes telling them the facts and encouraging them to trust their lives to Christ. But once they come to Christ, realize that God likely wants to use you to disciple your new Christian friends for weeks or months.

A MATTER OF STYLE

Historically, evangelism has been conducted in two different ways. First, there's the one-on-many style. On the day of Pentecost, Peter addressed a huge crowd in Jerusalem. He told them the facts, called for a decision, and three thousand people responded (Acts 2:14–41). The new believers were then absorbed into the church and discipled (verse 42). The one-on-many style of evangelism continues today whenever speakers, evangelists, pastors, or missionaries inform a crowd of listeners about Christ and seek to persuade them to trust Him.

Second, there's the one-on-one style of evangelism. Believers interact informally with non-Christian friends or classmates. They tell them about Christ and encourage them to trust Him as their Savior and Lord. You may be surprised to learn that far more people come to Christ as the result of one-on-one interaction than from mass crusades or evangelistic services.

There are also a few styles of one-on-one evangelism. One is often called friendship evangelism, and another could be labeled initiative evangelism.

In friendship evangelism, a Christian seeks to develop a relationship with a non-Christian over a period of time. Then, within the context of that friendship, the Christian shares the good news and invites his friend to trust Christ. Others favor initiative evangelism, believing that God always puts people around us who are ready to hear the good news and that long-term relationships are not necessary for these people to respond to the message. So their goal is to interact with non-Christians often, whether they are friends or just acquaintances, with the express purpose of sharing the gospel with them. Deeper relationships are developed during discipleship.

HOW SHOULD YOU SHARE YOUR FAITH?

When you think about it, there's really not much difference between friendship evangelism and initiative evangelism. A combination of the two is what we might call "friendship in evangelism." No matter how we approach people about Christ, the fact remains that someone must approach them, love them, and tell them about God's incredible purpose and plan for their lives.

Some of these individuals may be your friends. Others are only acquaintances. God wants you to share with both groups (1 Corinthians 9:19–22). No matter who you're with, here are some simple guidelines to help you share Christ:

1. Be sensitive to God's Spirit leading you. If you take a minute to think about it, you will see that God has already put people around you who don't know Him. Are you asking God to give you His eyes for these people? Are you catching the Holy Spirit's compassion and love for non-Christians? Will was gaining a concerned heart for Tony because of a prayer he prayed for him weeks earlier. Pray and ask God to give you His heart of compassion and to alert you to opportunities for sharing with those around you.

2. Be a friend to non-Christians. Do you tend to hang around only with those who have already trusted Christ? There are many good reasons for spending the majority of your fellowship time with other Christians. In fact, the Bible commands us to do so (Hebrews 10:25). But if you know and love non-Christians as well as Christians (not romantically, but as a concerned friend), you'll be in a better position to lead others to Christ.

Build relationships with non-Christians by looking for common interests. Affirm them in positive areas (don't affirm their drugs and drinking, for example, but affirm their good qualities). In this way, you'll be like Jesus, who was called a friend of sinners (Matthew 11:19).

3. Take the initiative, but be patient. Look for opportunities to tell others about God's love and forgiveness. Don't wait for them to ask you questions about spiritual things; *you* ask *them.* As you take the initiative, God will work through your words and the witness of your life to bring them to Christ.

Be patient as you share with others. Don't argue. Show them that you're a friend whether or not they agree with what you say or trust Christ personally.

Perhaps you've talked to God about your non-Christian friends like Will McConnell talked to God about Tony Ortiz: "God, you'd better do something." The Bible tells us that God has already done something, the most important something. Through the death and resurrection of Jesus Christ,

God has opened the doors from the kingdom of darkness to the kingdom of light. Now He's calling on you to do something: Join with Him to rescue the captives by prayerfully and lovingly telling them, persuading them, and discipling them.

Will and his friends are ready to respond to the challenge by committing themselves to God's rescue mission. And the creatures in Subsector 477 are gearing up to distract them like never before.

6

Commandos

Ratsbane's eyelid twitched constantly over the black bulb that was his right eye. He was still terribly distraught over his early failures on the Prime-evil Impulse Transducer. As a result, he was not the same swashbuckling mutant who had swaggered into the PIT cave six weeks earlier. Now every creak and snap in the conduits made his scaly skin crawl, suspecting a brigadier behind every boulder.

Ratsbane still shuddered at the memory of Maledictus entering the cave after the disastrous loss of Reggie Spencer and Krystal Wayne. Ratsbane had expected to be busted back to a maintenance runt or worse for foolishly challenging the brigadiers and disabling the PIT. But Maledictus slithered up to the foreman, Marplot, instead. The sector boss was blind with rage over Marplot's failure to keep the Westcastle youth group in check, holding him accountable for the havoc in the cave.

As the swan-python hissed and spat his disapproval, he slowly coiled his huge body around Marplot, who was petrified with fear. Gradually the crocodile-hog disappeared from view inside the massive rolls of python flesh. Then Maledictus began to squeeze. The sound from within the coils resembled a sack full of walnuts being shelled. The muscular grip tightened until Ratsbane heard a muffled *pop-squish.* Then Maledictus extended his swan head triumphantly and relaxed his grip. Marplot—that is, what was left of him—oozed and dribbled to the floor from between the coils. At the sight of his partner's demise, Stygios crumpled to the floor with a sickly moan.

A couple of runts scurried in, scooped Marplot's remains into a wheelbarrow, and scurried out to the recycling center. Like countless other punished mutants, he would be back on duty somewhere in hell in whatever form they could devise from the materials in the wheelbarrow.

Ratsbane staggered backward and collapsed on a pile of rocks for fear that he was the next ingredient in Maledictus' demon soup. But the swan head swooped low and said, "No need to worry yet, you foolish wretch. As much as I hate to admit it, I still need you and that other miserable excuse for a mutant. You've got spunk, Ratsbane. I haven't seen such hatred for the Enemy and the rebels in ages. And you've become surprisingly adept at operating the PIT in such a short time, even though your foolhardy confrontation of the brigadiers will cost us days in repairs." Ratsbane heaved a guarded sigh of relief.

"I'm taking over here personally, Ratsbane, effective immediately," Maledictus continued. "There'll be some changes. Those Westcastle brats and their brigadiers pose an extraordinary threat to my sector, and their threat must be countered with extraordinary measures. May I count on your unswerving loyalty to our cause?" Maledictus punctuated his question with a sudden flex of his powerful coils, obviously for Ratsbane's benefit.

Ratsbane tried to stifle an involuntary squeal of fright prompted by Maledictus' display. Then he scrambled to his feet and offered a rather clumsy salute.

Maledictus wasn't kidding, Ratsbane thought, surveying the PIT cave now, six weeks later. He had never seen such an array of firepower crammed into one cave. Not only had Subsector 477's original Prime-evil Impulse Transducer been fully repaired, but Maledictus had ordered the installation of three other slightly smaller PIT units. The once-spacious cave was now a crowded maze of flashing keyboards, glowing monitors, and humming conduits.

On Maledictus' orders, the three smaller PITs had been reconfigured specifically to track the activities of the Westcastle Community youth group. Ratsbane was assigned to one of them and Stygios to another. The third was available to Maledictus when he wasn't out terrorizing one of the several other less-active subsectors for which he was responsible.

The original giant PIT had been reprogrammed to keep the blinders securely in place on the rest of the Eisenhower High School student body. Ordinarily a three-demon operation, the oversized PIT was now manned by a veteran PIT operator Maledictus had conscripted from the Middle East division. Nefarius, a giant of a mutant bearing the head of a walrus on a gorilla's body, was able to span the entire keyboard with his huge arms, though his sausagelike fingers made for clumsy typing.

One question still nagged at Ratsbane as he climbed the scaffold for another long day of tracking the odious Westcastle youth group on his PIT. Subsector 477's beefed-up arsenal had been up and running for more than three weeks. Why hadn't Maledictus ordered Ratsbane and Stygios to open up on the rebels? If they are such a threat, why not start pounding them right away?

The Thursday-night discipleship group had been meeting regularly, and the two demons had kept Maledictus informed of everything, including Liz Cunningham's talk about rescuing the captives at Eisenhower. Ratsbane's fingers itched for battle. His hatred for the Enemy and the rebels mounted daily, pushing the pain of his earlier defeat from his memory. Yet Maledictus continued to hold back, except for a few trivial temptations to keep the apparatus warm.

"We will lull them into a false sense of security," the swan-python said when rejecting Ratsbane's most recent request to attack. "Soon they will be so holy-minded and self-confident that their defenses will weaken. Let the worldly attractions around them and the fleshly desires within them do their damage. When the time is right we will strike. Be patient, Ratsbane. Your day of glory will come."

☆ ☆ ☆

"United 272 to Denver tower," Captain McConnell spoke into his imaginary mic.

"This is Denver tower. Come in, United 272," Will answered himself in his best imitation of an air traffic controller.

"United 272 requests permission to land," the Captain said.

"United 272, you are clear to land on runway two-seven right."

The computer workstation where Will was "flying" gave evidence of the changes that had occurred in his life since the video party. Tacked to the wood panel just above his monitor were seven stick-up notes, each dated and containing a hand-printed verse from the Bible. Will got the idea during one of the discipleship meetings. Joy Akiyama had told the group that she selected one verse out of each day's Bible reading and used it as a theme for her day. She wrote the verse on a card and kept it with her, thinking about it and praying about it through the day. Will, who was struggling to come up with a similar plan, quickly adopted Joy's idea. He kept his verses above his computer, where he spent a good many hours of his week.

Will was so absorbed in his Saturday night flight to Denver's Stapleton airport that he didn't hear the rustle in the bushes outside the large window next to his computer. After all, the captain of a 727 has to be focused, especially when his cargo is the Chicago Bears, whom Will was transporting to Denver to play the Broncos. But the heavy metallic tap on the window pane jolted him back to reality. His startled jump jiggled the Mac's controls and sent his 727 into a violent turn toward Wyoming.

Will jumped again when he saw what was at the window: the barrel of a rifle that, thankfully, was pointed upward instead of at him. Behind the rifle was what looked to Will like a bush with eyes. No, it wasn't a bush; it was a person who looked like a bush. Finally, Will sighed with relief. "I can't believe it," he mumbled, opening the window. "Come on in."

It wasn't until Jason clambered over the sill that Will could fully appreciate Jason's get-up. Tonight he was dressed in camouflage-print army fatigues, jackboots, pack, and helmet. His face was smeared brown and green with grease paint. The only unofficial-looking part of his uniform was the rifle, an old, partially rusted BB gun.

Will chuckled as he scanned his friend's uniform from helmet to boots and back again. "And the winner of this year's Oscar for the best costume for doing nothing on a Saturday night is—ta-ta-da—Jason Withers."

As always, Jason appreciated the recognition. "But I'm not doing nothing," he insisted, removing his helmet and slipping out of his pack. "I've got a great idea for our discipleship group."

"Don't tell me you want us to dress in costume every week."

"No, the army uniform isn't the idea, it just conveys the idea. It got your attention, didn't it?"

"Yeah, it got my attention so well that the Chicago Bears are headed toward the Canadian border." Will tapped the commands on his Mac to abort his flight. "This better be good, Jason—real good."

Ten minutes later Will was shaking his head in wonder. "Jason, you're unreal. That's a dynamite idea. I think we should tell the whole group on Thursday night. Better yet, let's tell the group before Thursday and surprise the Cunninghams." Jason agreed. Then they exchanged high and low fives just like they'd won the Super Bowl.

Amber's date with the student body vice-president was a disaster. She had let Vince talk her into going to a movie that she knew she shouldn't see. Then after the movie they ended up at the pizza place where Tony Ortiz's latest girlfriend worked, and Tony and his crowd were there. Tony was half drunk, and his rowdy behavior brought back some bad memories for Amber. Then to top off the evening, Vince got a little too free with his hands when Amber consented to a quick kiss good-night. *That's it!* she decided as she closed the front door and switched off the porch light. *No more dates with non-Christian guys.* Her disappointing evening had left her on the verge of tears.

She had just reached her room when her phone rang.

"Hi, Amber. This is Will. I hope I'm not calling too late."

"Hi, Will. No, I just got home." Amber was trying to cover the slight quaver in her voice as she spoke. "What's happening?"

"Jason and I were talking tonight about a great idea for our group. We want to get everybody together tomorrow after church to talk about it, okay?"

"Sure, I'll be there," she answered, sniffling slightly.

"Hey, Amber, are you all right?"

Will's point-blank question caught Amber off guard. After her evening with Vince, she suddenly appreciated Will's caring friendship. She cried a little and talked in discreet generalities about her evening. Will listened patiently, then told her everything would be okay. He told her he'd pray for her before he went to sleep. Amber hung up the phone wishing she had a boyfriend who cared for her the way Will did.

Duane and Liz didn't notice at first how strangely the Thursday-night gang was dressed and how curiously they were grinning at each other. Jason's fatigues, boots, and helmet were no great shock considering his penchant for the wild and crazy. But then the Cunninghams realized that everybody was dressed in khaki, olive drab, or navy blue. Many were wearing shirts or jackets with military insignias. The eight disciples looked like models in a tacky fashion show at the local army surplus store.

"There's a reason for the way we look," Will explained after Liz finally asked about their costumes. "What you said last week about God's rescue mission really hit home with us." Will explained briefly his insight at the football game, but refrained from using names so he wouldn't embarrass Reggie or Amber. A few others also stated that they had been thinking seriously about the kids at school who were still in darkness.

"Jason came up with a great idea," Will continued, "that we think will help us do something about the kids at Ike who need to be rescued from the darkness. We are a discipleship group, and that's helping us. But we also need to be a team of kids reaching out to liberate others at school. We're willing to do that, but we don't exactly know how to go about it. We'd like you to train us so we can be part of God's rescue mission at Eisenhower."

Then Jason took over. He stood, and in the voice of a gravely voiced drill sergeant barked, "Ten-hut!" The rest of the group jumped up and stiffened in mock military attention. "And so, Commander and Mrs. Cunningham, allow me to present for your inspection the Liberation Commandos of Eisenhower High School." As Jason snapped a salute, Will stepped forward and presented Duane with a clean but old air force shirt, and Amber gave a well-worn navy summer jersey to Liz. The Cunninghams played the role to the hilt, accepting their "uniforms" and saluting in return.

After a minute of laughter and silly saluting, Duane had everybody sit down. "I really think God has something great in mind for us," he said seriously. "He's also been speaking to me this week about His rescue mission. I work with a lot of guys on the construction site who are just as lost as the kids at Eisenhower.

"As Liz and I prayed and talked this week, we realized that God was directing us to launch our group into a Bible study that will equip us to become a liberating force in our community. And so, Liberation Commandos, we accept your appointment, effective immediately."

The Inside Story: Recruited to Liberate

What words would you use to identify yourself as a Christian? Would you think in terms that describe your position in Christ: saved, redeemed, born again, justified? Would you use your church affiliation to mark your identity: Baptist, Catholic, Methodist, Presbyterian?

Will, Jason, Amber, and the other members of the Westcastle group have made an important discovery about their identity as Christians. It relates to their understanding that the majority of the kids in their school and community are still lost without Christ. They no longer see themselves merely as growing Christians but as liberators. They know they must actively seek to evangelize and disciple others. They call themselves the Liberation Commandos because they know that God has summoned all believers to join in His mission to liberate those in darkness from the power of sin and Satan.

GOD WANTS YOU INVOLVED

You won't find the words "Liberation Commandos" in the Bible, but God's Word clearly reveals that He intends for us to be involved in His rescue operation. There are several reasons why you should consider yourself a Liberation Commando in your school and community.

1. Jesus has called you to be a liberator. Jesus called His first disciples to be witnesses at home (for them that was Jerusalem) and to the ends of their earth (Acts 1:8). He also said to them, "Come, follow me . . . and I will make you fishers of men" (Matthew 4:19).

If you're like a lot of Christians, you like the idea of following Jesus. It's great to have a leader you can trust, who protects you and gives you wisdom so you can make right decisions. But as He did with His original disciples, Christ also calls us to be witnesses (communicating the good news) and fishers of men (rescuing others out of darkness). We should enjoy our relationship with God. But God also intends for us to share that relationship with others.

2. The non-Christians around you need to be liberated. No matter how successful and happy people may appear, if they have not trusted Christ, they are headed in only one direction: eternal separation from God. Remember Jesus' words of compassion for the people around you who are chained in darkness. They are "harassed and helpless, like sheep without a shepherd" (Matthew 9:36).

3. You are important to God's rescue plan. Someone needs to tell your friends and acquaintances the good news. The apostle Paul asked, "How can they believe in the one of whom they have not heard? And how can they hear without someone preaching to them?" (Romans 10:14). God wants to use you!

4. *You want to rescue others because God rescued you.* Think about your life before you trusted Christ. Think about what your life would be like today without Him. Aren't you grateful that God in His love has invited you to be His child? Doesn't your appreciation for God's love and your love for Him encourage you to want to join Him in inviting others to trust Him?

Paul said that he was compelled by Christ's love to join Him in His rescue mission (2 Corinthians 5:14). The better you understand how much God loves you and what He has done for you, the more you will want to reflect His love by helping others find Him.

ROADBLOCKS TO BEING A LIBERATOR

Even though God's Word clearly directs us to rescue those in darkness by communicating the good news about Christ, many Christians are not personally involved in God's rescue mission. Why? They offer at least four excuses. Are you hiding behind one or more of these excuses instead of boldly moving out to fulfill your rescue assignment?

1. *"I'm not capable."* Some Christians are not involved in reaching out and sharing with others because they don't think they possess the ability or gifts to reach out to others.

This is a common feeling, but it's not legitimate. If you feel this way, listen to what the Scriptures say to you: "For we are God's workmanship, created in Christ Jesus to do good works, which God prepared in advance for us to do" (Ephesians 2:10).

Being God's workmanship means that He has given you special abilities, talents, and gifts. You are uniquely equipped for what God wants you to do. Furthermore, to be created in Christ Jesus means that God has given you a new nature and His Holy Spirit to provide the power to use the abilities He has given. And He has good works already lined up for you to do.

So you can't say, "I'm just not capable to be used by God." That's an insult to all God has done to prepare you to be used in rescuing others. Be bold and step out on what God has done to make you capable.

2. *"I'm not living a very good Christian life."* Some Christians can get tangled up in sin themselves. Unconfessed sin can pile high within them. They aren't walking in the power of the Holy Spirit. They don't share with others because they don't have much to share about.

If this is your excuse, you must realize that your condition isn't God's fault. He has made every provision for you to enjoy a rich, Spirit-filled life. You need to claim what He has already provided. Confess your sin, be filled with the Spirit, and allow Him to lead your life daily. You don't have to be perfect to join the Liberation Commandos, but you must be learning to walk by depending on God.

3. *"I don't know what to say to non-Christians."* You may think you don't have the training or education to communicate your faith and encourage others to trust Christ. But you also didn't have the training to drive a car when you reached the legal driving age. So did you stay home moping to yourself because you didn't know how to drive? Of course not. You didn't let ignorance keep you off the road for long.

Like driving, knowing what to say to others about Christ comes through training and practice. You need to acquire the necessary knowledge and skills. The rest of this book will equip you with the basic tools to be a liberator, including what to say and how to say it.

4. *"I'm afraid of how non-Christians will respond."* Fear is one of the primary roadblocks that keeps us from sharing Christ with others. Satan and the world around us both generate fear. They trick us into believing that what people think is more important than the message of liberation we have to share with them. As long as you focus on yourself

instead of others (remember the ME button on the PIT?), you will be ineffective as a liberator.

Paul wrote to Timothy: "For God did not give us a spirit of timidity, but a spirit of power, of love and of self-discipline" (2 Timothy 1:7). If you are afraid of how non-Christians will respond, you need to confess your sin and trust God to give you His confidence. Then, as you take steps of faith to talk with others, you will discover God's courage in your life—just when you need it. In fact, you usually won't experience God's power until you put yourself in a position where you need it.

ARE YOU READY TO BE A LIBERATOR?

Joining God in His rescue operation is a privilege. God doesn't have to use you to reach your non-Christian friends. He could as easily use angels, chimpanzees, or granite boulders. But instead He has chosen to involve you in His mission. He wants you to experience the fulfillment of being His instrument in your school and community.

The name "Liberation Commandos" is appropriate for a group of rescuers like Will and his friends. A commando is a member of a small, well-trained force sent to work behind enemy lines. The nature of God's rescue plan demands that we aggressively penetrate Satan's territory in order to find the captives and lead them into the light and freedom of God's kingdom.

The Bible clearly states that, even though Satan was defeated through the death and resurrection of Jesus Christ, he does not give up his captives without a fight. As illustrated in the fictional description of Ratsbane and the Prime-evil Impulse Transducer, the world, the flesh, and the devil are working against your efforts to liberate your friends. You must be ready to arm yourself with the weapons God provides and join the battle if you hope to be successful in the rescue.

By weapons, of course, we're not talking about howitzers, stealth bombers, "smart" bombs, or machine guns. Paul reminds us that the battle we're engaged in is spiritual, so the weapons we use are also spiritual (2 Corinthians 10:3–4). What are the weapons in our spiritual arsenal that will allow us to invade Satan's territory and rescue his captives? Well, the Liberation Commandos of Eisenhower High School are about to be briefed on this very question.

7

Heavy Artillery

The cafeteria was crowded and noisy as Will, Jason, and Amber huddled around one end of a long table. This was their first meeting as a prayer group on campus, and they all felt a little self-conscious about praying where other kids could overhear or interrupt them. So they ate their lunches without saying much at all about prayer or the Liberation Commandos.

Will glanced at Amber as she picked at her small salad. He wished he could pinpoint exactly how he felt about her. Since their recommitment to Christ, they often talked and prayed with each other like good friends. At other times her rising-star status in Ike's social solar system made him a little jealous. When Amber was orbiting with the ASB officers or the rally, Will didn't even think she knew him. At those times he felt no more important to her than a fly speck on a passing meteorite.

But when he was this close to her, Will wanted badly to be more than a friend or a fly speck to Amber. He wasn't sure if he loved her, but he sure loved being near her— seeing her, hearing her, and sometimes touching her. He was a lot quicker these days about confessing and turning off his lustful thoughts about her. But of all the girls Will knew, if he had to choose one to take to a movie (if and when he decided to start dating), to invite to the prom, to share his first kiss, and to have sex with—after they were married, of course—it would be Amber.

Will also studied Jason as his zany friend arranged a row of French fries on his slice of pizza, then folded it over and took a huge bite. Jason still made him laugh a lot. But in the weeks since the video party, he and Jason had become like brothers. And Jason's spiritual insights had amazed Will. The Liberation Commandos, only a week old, had been his idea. And the Commandos had already accomplished something for the discipleship group nothing else had accomplished: It brought them together at school for prayer.

Will was still shaking his head in amazement over Jason's contribution to the first Commandos meeting last night. Duane had been talking to the group about the two major weapons the Commandos should use in liberating non-Christians from the darkness: prayer and sharing the truth of the gospel.

That's when Jason spoke up. "The Liberation Commandos are kind of like the coalition army that fought for the liberation of Kuwait in the Persian Gulf War. I did a report in history last week about it. In the first phase of the war, the combined air forces bombed the enemy's positions every day for weeks." Jason paused to interject his own sound effects for exploding bombs. "When the ground assault started, our troops won easily because the enemy was heavily damaged and disorganized, physically and psychologically.

"In our rescue operation, prayer is like that air assault. As we pray for kids in the darkness, God's power bombs Satan's territory." He threw in a few more exploding bomb sounds. "Then when we move in and share the good news with kids who don't know Christ, they'll understand and trust Him because the enemy's power is broken."

Will remembered how quiet the Cunninghams' living room was after Jason's simple illustration. Finally Duane said, "Wow, Jason, that's fantastic! I guess we'd better start launching some prayer sorties for the kids at Eisenhower."

Will also thought about how his life had changed in the weeks since the campout. He was taking time almost every day to read his Bible. He also had established a prayer list. He prayed every night (when he didn't forget or wasn't too tired) for his mother and the Liberation Commandos. He had even begun praying for his father, who to his knowledge was not a Christian. And for a week now, since Jason and Duane called the Commandos to launch a prayer offensive, Will had developed a short list of non-Christian kids to pray for—including Tony Ortiz.

Amber's touch on his arm snapped Will out of his reverie. "Will, if we're going to pray like we're supposed to, we'd better go somewhere else. We only have about ten minutes before the end of lunch." Jason agreed that the cafeteria wasn't the best place to follow through with their commitment to begin praying together for the liberation of Eisenhower High School.

The outdoor quad area, where most students ate lunch in the balmy early fall and late spring, was almost deserted on this gray, forty-degree November day. The three Commandos found a bench away from the walkway. They scrunched close together with their hands jammed into their coats.

Jason prayed first. He closed his eyes, but he didn't bow his head because he didn't want the kids watching from the cafeteria to think he was praying. "Lord, thank You for everything You've done in our youth group since the campout. And thank You for wanting to use us to help liberate other kids at Ike from Satan's kingdom. We pray that You will—"

"Amber, I'm glad I found you." Hillary, a bubbly blonde member of Amber's rally squad, didn't realize she was interrupting a prayer sortie. She began talking to Amber as if Will and Jason were wooden statues on the bench. "We're supposed to meet with Mrs. Anthony after seventh period.

She's agreed to help us put together a special routine for the first playoff game tomorrow."

Hillary squeezed in between Will and Amber on the bench and began describing in great detail the routine she thought would be best. Amber kept smiling and nodding. Will and Jason made faces at each other behind the girls' backs.

After Hillary finally left, Jason was barely able to complete one more sentence of his prayer before the bell rang. They each felt a twinge of disappointment and failure, and their faces mirrored their feelings. Will didn't want to leave his friends on such a discouraging note. "Well, I guess our first mission was scrubbed before we could drop any bombs," he said, smiling. "But let's take off again Monday at 1200 hours and see if we can at least get to the target. Okay?"

Amber nodded and Jason gave a confident thumbs-up sign. Then they headed off to class.

The first week of prayer sorties by the Liberation Commandos had caused only mild alarm in Subsector 477. Lord Maledictus, who was spending most of his time monitoring the Westcastle situation personally, continued to urge his underlings toward restraint. "Those play-acting soldiers don't have a clue about the immensity of the task they have undertaken," he hissed to Ratsbane and Stygios. "They expect to say a few prayers and then watch the student body suddenly drop to its knees in repentance. But watch them fold when nothing happens right away. They'll get too busy with other activities and forget to meet together to pray. When they kneel down alone in their rooms, they'll get tired and distracted and fall asleep. And while they're struggling against the influences of the world and the flesh, our transmissions will further distract them with delightful temptations. Commandos—ha! They're no different than other kids who started the same way. They don't have what it takes for the long haul."

Ratsbane received Maledictus' pep talk with only guarded optimism. Day by day he watched Will, Jason, and Amber get together at noon to launch another of their prayer sorties. At the same time, Buster, Reggie, and Krystal met to pray in Buster's car, and Darcelle and Joy had a prayer meeting going in a deserted corner of the library.

As Maledictus predicted, the prayers of the little Commando groups were not very profound. But the growing volume of noise in the stacks of conduits aimed at Eisenhower High School kept Ratsbane's eye twitching rapidly.

"Steady, Ratsbane," Maledictus urged whenever he saw him pacing the scaffold and ducking sporadic outbursts of sparks and gravel. "I assure you that these little prayer groups won't last till Christmas."

Ratsbane also tracked the eight youthful Commandos when they were attempting solo prayer sorties at home. Maledictus had been right about the power of worldly attractions and the kids' own fleshly thoughts and feelings to swerve them away from prayer.

Ratsbane was rather proud of his contribution that kept Will from praying for a list of captives one night. The demon watched as he labored through a pile of homework, intending to save a half-hour before bedtime for his nightly Bible reading and prayer. Ratsbane knew that Will hadn't played on his Mac for a couple of days due to homework and devotions. So the demon tapped out a subtle combination with the ME button that suggested to Will, "You've had a tough day. You deserve a break before quiet time. How about a nice flight from chilly Westcastle to sun-drenched Miami?" Then he watched with satisfaction as Will got so involved in his flight that he lost track of time. He barely stayed awake long enough for a Now-I-lay-me-down-to-sleep prayer.

Ratsbane had witnessed and encouraged similar lapses in each of the Commandos. Jason didn't watch the "skin" channel anymore, but his old habits occasionally prompted him to rationalize a "harmless" R-rated film on one of the movie channels. And there was usually just enough sex and nudity included to keep Jason distracted from serious prayer for hours, even days.

Amber's schedule was so full and her parents so protective of her time that her quiet time was sometimes overlooked. With the Eisenhower Generals still winning games in the state football tournament, she was kept busy with the rally team after school and on Saturdays. And in Amber's quiet moments, Ratsbane's devious reminders of her previous rebellion against the Enemy and her parents sometimes preoccupied her with questions about her forgiveness, leaving little time to pray for her list of friends.

But as the month of November wore on, Ratsbane began to wonder if Maledictus' confidence about the collapse of the praying Commandos was little more than wishful thinking.

"Sir, each of the kids has experienced setbacks in their commitment to pray as you predicted," he reported to his superior one day. "But they keep rebounding. They confess their failures to the Enemy and to each other. They keep refilling their inner power packs with the Enemy's Spirit. And they keep praying. One of the miserable humans even thought to ask the pastor to make their group a subject of prayer in the church, until I . . ."—his bulging eyes blinked with pride—". . . until I distracted him at just the right moment. The conduits aren't exploding, but they are cracking and chipping. Maintenance is having difficulty keeping them patched together. Even Nefarius admits that his blinding apparatus, which is attached to hundreds of captives at the school, is being affected. What shall we do?"

Maledictus slithered back and forth nervously in the narrow space between the PITs as Ratsbane spoke. "Those wretches are holding together better than I expected," he grumbled. "It's time to increase the power. Take advantage of every worldly interest and fleshly weakness they have. Their prayer attacks must be stopped!"

It was the command Ratsbane had been awaiting for weeks. His rekindled anger and hatred toward the Enemy and the Commandos had all but obliterated his earlier failure. He had pushed the memory of the brigadiers to the farthest corner of his twisted mind. He eagerly climbed the scaffold and prepared to power up.

☆   ☆   ☆

Reggie Spencer had come up with the idea at the Commandos meeting the Thursday before Thanksgiving. "You remember that See-You-at-the-Pole thing back in September? Where a bunch of us Christian kids gathered around the flagpole for prayer and a visible witness? Maybe the eight of us together should do something like that again."

At first the group applauded Reggie's idea. But then they couldn't decide how to do it, and soon they were bickering about when to do it. "Hey, wait a minute!" Duane interrupted as the normally cohesive Commandos snipped at each other. "It sounds like we're getting increased resistance from the enemy. Let's stop and pray right now that God's plan won't be foiled by our selfishness or Satan's interference."

The Commandos sheepishly admitted that Duane was right, and a few apologies were exchanged. Then Duane led the group in prayer. "Lord, we know from the resistance we have experienced tonight that our prayer sorties are taking a toll on the enemy. We stand against our pride and selfishness and the distractions around us. We resist the enemy's attempts to place us under siege and keep us from completing our mission. Keep leading us into victory as we work with You in Your rescue mission."

The rest of the Liberation Commandos joined Duane in a hearty amen. Then they quickly made plans for a "prayer walk" around the school ending with a "prayer stand" at the flagpole during lunch period on the day before Thanksgiving. If they could have seen what was happening in Subsector 477 they would have cheered themselves hoarse.

The Inside Story:
Tapping into
Prayer Power

Leave it to Jason to come up with a clever illustration for the two elements of the liberation of those in darkness: the Persian Gulf War. It was the war we watched on television every day like the episodes of a tragic, gut-wrenching mini-series—except that it was very real.

For over a month, coalition forces bombed Iraqi command and control centers and military installations in Iraq and in occupied Kuwait. Tens of thousands of sorties were flown, striking preplanned enemy targets with uncanny accuracy. Then, in less than a week, a well-strategized ground offensive swept into enemy territory and drove the Iraqi army out of Kuwait.

As Jason said, the persistent, repeated air strikes involving thousands of planes reminds us of the critical importance of prayer in the evangelism of non-Christians. The air strikes disrupted the enemy's communication, disabled its offensive power, and decimated its resources. Similarly, when you pray you are disrupting, disabling, and decimating Satan's power in the lives of your non-Christian friends suffering under his occupation.

The swift and effective ground war that followed re-minds us of the second element in liberating the captives of sin: sharing the gospel of truth with those in darkness and persuading them to claim their freedom by trusting Christ. As effective as the air campaign was, it wasn't enough. Ground troops had to march into the occupied territory, finish the job, and proclaim freedom to the captives. In the same way, along with fervent, persistent prayer, you need an effective strategy for sharing the good news with your non-Christian friends—the good news that Jesus Christ has set them free.

Both of those PowerLinks are necessary. When you pray, you lay hold of God's unlimited "airpower"; when you share the truth with a non-Christian, you march into enemy territory, proclaiming freedom to the captives.

In this chapter we will focus on prayer, the first vital element of evangelism. In the following chapters we will discuss the second vital element, sharing the truth of the good news with others.

UNDERSTANDING PRAYER

Does your understanding of prayer come from your childhood, from listening to grownups talk to God in thees and thous or six-syllable theological words you'd never heard before?

Relax. Prayer is simply talking to God about your thoughts, feelings, and concerns. And God really does un-derstand modern English (including usage that doesn't come from a dictionary). And you can be totally confident that God hears you when you pray. In fact, God eagerly waits for you to come to Him in prayer. You are His child, and He values every minute you spend with Him!

Why is prayer so great? Here are some important an-swers.

1. Prayer helps us focus on God. It puts our eyes on God and helps us know Him better. The psalmist said, "Look to the Lord and his strength; seek his face always" (Psalm 105:4). When we take time to pray, we "unplug" our minds from the television and the CD player and "plug in" to God.

2. Prayer is intimacy with God. When you pray, you discover what it means to be intimate with God. The Bible says that when Moses entered the tabernacle, "The Lord would speak to Moses face to face, as a man speaks with his friend" (Exodus 33:11). *That* is what happens in prayer. You become friends with God. You develop more than an acquaintance with Him; He becomes a deep, intimate, personal friend who loves you unconditionally. As you relate to God in prayer, you will stay in tune with His heartbeat for you and the captives around you.

3. Prayer is a vital weapon in spiritual battle. We have seen from Will and Amber's lives that spiritual conflict is a reality. We face it every day. And prayer is the "big gun" in our spiritual arsenal.

In Ephesians 6:10–20, the apostle Paul lists the armor we are to use in fighting the spiritual battle. He says we are to wear our faith as a shield against Satan's flaming arrows, put on the helmet of salvation, and use the sword of the Spirit which is God's Word (verses 16–17).

Then Paul lists prayer, not once but four times, as it applies to spiritual warfare. He says, "Pray in the Spirit on all occasions with all kinds of prayers. . . . Be alert and always keep on praying for all the saints [Christians]. Pray also for me . . . so that I will fearlessly make known the mystery of the gospel. . . . Pray that I may declare it fearlessly, as I should" (verses 18–20).

When we pray, God takes action! Your prayers for your non-Christian friends paralyze Satan as God works in their lives. He prepares your friends to receive the message that He gives you the strength to share.

PRAYING WITH CONFIDENCE

God already intends to do some incredible things on your campus and in your community. When you pray, God puts you in touch and in harmony with what he intends to accomplish.

When you know God has a plan for your school and for reaching your friends, you can pray with real confidence. God has given you some radical promises to claim, for example: "Only ask, and I will give you all the nations of the world" (Psalm 2:8 TLB). To bring God's promise a little closer to home, you may want to paraphrase it like this: Only ask, and I will give you your football team (or your rally squad, your chemistry class, the two guys who sit next to you on the bus every day).

God's promise is to give; our responsibility is to ask in prayer. Here are several vital guidelines to help you ask confidently and receive what God has promised.

1. Keep depending on Christ. Jesus said: "If you remain in me and my words remain in you, ask whatever you wish, and it will be given you" (John 15:7). What does it mean to remain in Christ? It's another way to describe walking in the Spirit. Practically speaking, you show your willingness to remain in Christ as you confess known sin and invite the Holy Spirit to fill your life.

You allow Christ's words to remain in you by getting God's Word into you, by reading it, studying it, memorizing it, and discussing it. His Word remains in you as you make it part of your life through obedience—by doing what it says. As you live day by day depending on Christ, you can ask Him to break Satan's grip on your friends and prepare them to receive the good news, and He will do it.

2. Pray specifically. A lot of Christians pray in fuzzy generalities, so that they have little idea of what they're asking or what answers to look for. Get specific with God as you pray for your non-Christian friends.

First, pray for specific people. Write down the names of the people to whom God is directing you to witness (parents, friends, classmates, teammates, etc.). If it's a long list, break it up and pray for a different list of names each day.

Second, pray specifically about what you want God to do. One idea is to select a Bible verse about salvation and claim it for the people on your list. You might use John 17:2: "For you [God the Father] granted him [Jesus the Son] authority over all people that he might give eternal life to all those you have given him." You might pray, "Thank You, Lord, that you have authority over my lab partner, Vickie. I ask You to break Satan's power over her and prepare her to receive the gospel so she may have eternal life."

3. *Pray according to God's revealed will.* There may be some things you pray about for which God's will is not clear, so you're not sure how you should pray. But praying for the salvation of your non-Christian friends is not one of those areas. God's will regarding their salvation is crystal clear: He doesn't want any of them to be lost (2 Peter 3:9). When you pray that your friends will be delivered from the darkness and trust Christ, be confident that you are asking for something that God has clearly stated is His will.

4. *Expect God to answer your prayers.* Jesus promised: "If you believe, you will receive whatever you ask for in prayer" (Matthew 21:22). As you pray for the non-Christians on your list, begin to see them from the perspective of what God wants and what you have prayed. Act on your belief by preparing to share the good news with your friends when the opportunity is right. Expect that God is going to answer your prayers and liberate your friends—perhaps through you.

GETTING STARTED

You may think about how wonderful it will be when your non-Christian friends trust Christ. But thinking nice thoughts isn't the same as praying. Prayer is an action.

Prayer is taking time to talk to God specifically about what you're thinking. Here are some ways to become an active pray-er:

- Go to God regularly to pray. Begin by thanking and praising Him for His greatness.
- Pray alone over your personal list of non-Christian friends.
- Pray regularly for non-Christians with a small group of friends. For example, Will, Jason, and Amber have become prayer "triplets" at Eisenhower.
- Take time in your church or Christian student meeting to pray together about your witness to non-Christians.
- Join with other Christians at school for a prayer walk around or through your campus. We're not talking about a noisy, showy religious procession. Just get together to walk around the areas where kids congregate: cafeteria, auditorium, classrooms, bleachers. As you walk, pray silently for God's power to be released so that many captives may be freed and trust Christ.

Prayer is the big gun, the ultimate spiritual weapon. As you pray, God prepares you to do what He has called you to do. But as you begin to pray for your non-Christian friends you must be aware that they also need to hear and respond to the good news. What exactly do they need to know about God, Jesus, and salvation? Interestingly, the Liberation Commandos have been asking the same question.

8

Turkey Day Flop

Subsector 477 was looking more like a gravel pit every day. The steady barrage of seemingly insignificant prayers launched by the Commandos for their captive friends was gradually chipping away at the PIT complex. The floor of the cave was covered with an uneven sea of shattered rock and frayed cables. Each of the four Prime-evil Impulse Transducers wore a mantle of sand and rock slivers from the disintegrating conduits. And the swirling dust made the cave even darker than usual despite hundreds of flashing buttons and dials and scores of glowing monitors.

The cave was also very crowded. Replacement parts—giant spools of cable and stacks of stone conduit and panels—littered the gravel sea. In addition to the four PITs and their operators, the cave swarmed with squirmy maintenance runts trying desperately to keep up with the repairs on the crumbling apparatus. Their ladders and scaffolds were propped everywhere. The demons could hardly operate their controls without reaching around or stepping over one or two of the little runts.

Ratsbane was in a particularly foul mood this Wednesday morning. True, last week he had increased his power output briefly in response to Maledictus' order. And he had succeeded in encouraging a little disharmony among the

Commandos as they tried to plan their prayer walk. But, disgustingly true to form, Duane, the radical youth leader, prayed, and Ratsbane had to power down before the torrent from the prayer completely disabled the PIT. As a result, Ratsbane had been running at half-power while several sections of cable and conduit above him were being replaced. The runts had just completed the job when Maledictus called Ratsbane, Stygios, and Nefarius together for a conference.

"Those contemptible Commandos are banding together for their prayer walk at noon today, and I don't like the looks of it," he hissed hotly. "Nefarius, their prayers will be aimed at hundreds of captives blinded by your apparatus. Keep the darkness flowing to their blinders." The walrus-gorilla mutant assented with a grunt that sounded like a belch in an echo chamber.

"Ratsbane and Stygios, you work on the Commandos. Most of them are fearful, self-conscious, and embarrassed about what they're going to do. Others are doubtful that their prayers will make a difference in their school. Luckily, their fleshly nature is providing all those distractions for us. But keep supplementing them with ME-impulse combinations while I blindside them with a few startling impressions that will make them forget all about prayer."

The three underlings turned to assume their posts and program their coordinates. "One more thing," Maledictus added. They turned to face him again. "This is just a prayer walk, not an evangelistic crusade. I don't expect any brigadiers in this engagement. Nevertheless, keep your eyes open for blue and white, and mind your tempers. I'd rather report the loss of a few rebels than the destruction of four transducers and their imbecilic operators." Maledictus flexed, and his intent was not lost on Ratsbane and Stygios.

The prayer walk began at the beginning of the lunch period. The eight Commandos met at the front gate of the school and set out together to walk its perimeter. To the casual observer they looked like a pack of kids out for a noon stroll. But Ratsbane knew better. He couldn't hear their silent prayers, of course; only the Enemy could. But the ant-toad mutant knew that they were up to no good. He eyed them cautiously and his stubby hands steadily drummed the controls, sending a stream of subtle impulses to the surface.

"That's it, Commandos, look around," Ratsbane muttered hatefully. "Yes, your fellow students are watching you. They think you're nuts. And besides, your prayers are going nowhere. Give up and go get some lunch."

Meanwhile, using his beak and the tip of his tail on the keyboard, Maledictus programmed a wicked concoction of tempting thoughts and shrewdly watched for windows of opportunity. Jason's attention was suddenly diverted by his stomach growling for pizza and French fries. Maledictus saw the distraction and fired a horrible suggestion at Jason's idle mind. The temptation combined a scene from a raunchy movie he'd watched once with a lustful thought about Darcelle, who was walking in front of him.

Maledictus watched as Jason fondled the idea for a few moments. But then he caught himself, silently confessed his thought, and brushed it from his mind. A string of flame zapped down the conduit and blew a handful of chunks out of the panel in front of Maledictus. The swan-python spat a curse and slammed the panel with his whiplike tail.

The same thing happened when he aimed a hateful thought at Joy's mind and when he peppered Reggie's thoughts with exaggerated memories of his sexual adventures with Krystal before they became Christians. The PIT-generated missiles seemed to bounce off the kids like they were wearing armor.

Once the Commandos completed the perimeter they turned toward the school and concluded in a prayer stand, their hands joined in a circle, around the flagpole.

Ratsbane stiffened as the silent praying seemed to become more intense and focused. *They're naming names! I bet they're even praying for specific classrooms and clubs!* he grumbled to himself. Gradually he eased the power lever upward. His fingers danced across the keyboard searching for disrupting combinations. He cursed the Commandos' fleshly natures for being so punchless at a time like this. But the praying continued.

Ratsbane spat out a venomous curse. "They're doing it." He cursed again. "Oh, Satan forbid. I think it's happening."

"What?" Stygios shouted over the din of moaning conduits, splintering rock, and sizzling sections of cable. "What's happening? What are they doing?"

"The PowerLink, you fool. They're making the link."

"Whaddya mean, 'PowerLink'?"

"You stupid beakhead," Ratsbane growled. "You don't get it, do you? Hell has no fear of 'praying,' of spineless Christians mumbling wish lists to a far-off God. It's *the link* that scares the—that scares us. It's when they link up with the power of *the Holy One—*"

Ratsbane narrowly dodged a sharp blow from Maledictus' beak.

"I should have snatched your tongue out of your head," Maledictus said as fountains of sparks and flame showered them from exploding panels. Ratsbane, Stygios, and Maledictus separated once more and began madly beating the controls.

But the worst punishment was being suffered by Nefarius. The prayers of the Commandos were deluging the captives under his control. Hundreds of lines to the surface buzzed loudly, and the conduits glowed orange as the blinding capacity of the PIT was being eroded. The thunderous, sustained roar from the power clash began to vibrate his PIT off its foundation. Huge sections of conduit shuddered and fell away.

"We're under siege!" Nefarius bellowed hysterically as he attacked the keyboard with his tree-trunk arms.

Then, without warning, *boom!* The sound of the explosion flattened Ratsbane's lone antenna against his dust-covered dome. A split-second later, a black, hairy blur with tusks whistled over him like a cannonball. Nefarius caromed off the cave wall with a thud and crashed into the conduits above Maledictus. Like bowling pins after a strike, a dozen or more large sections of conduit flew into the air on impact and rained down on the console and its stunned operator.

Ratsbane and Stygios worked feverishly to clear away the pile of conduits over Maledictus and extricate Nefarius from a tangle of cables. As they did, the monitors that were still working showed the Liberation Commandos leaving the flagpole together and walking to the cafeteria for lunch.

"That was only a prayer walk," a dazed Maledictus mumbled as his underlings pulled him from the rubble by his tail. "Satan help us if those kids learn how to talk *about* the Enemy as effectively as they talk *to* Him." Meanwhile the damaged, smoldering PIT that shot Nefarius across the cave glowed an eerie blue-white.

Amber hadn't quite finished her pumpkin pie when she heard the telephone ringing in her room. Her father glanced at her with that can't-it-wait-until-after-dinner look. She excused herself from the table, saying she'd tell the caller she was eating.

When Amber heard Tony's voice, she gripped the receiver tightly. A flood of conflicting feelings washed over her. Not knowing which of her feelings might come out if she spoke, she said nothing.

"I know I'm probably interrupting your Thanksgiving dinner, but I just had to call you. I need to see you. I'm not talking about a date or anything like that. I just have some things I need to talk about."

Amber listened closely. *He doesn't sound drunk, not even a little. But what does he want with me, especially since he knows I've changed?* Tony paused for a response, but Amber remained silent.

"This may not work, but I was hoping I could come over later this afternoon, just for a few minutes. Would that be all right?"

Amber hoped her emotions weren't setting her up, but she sensed something in Tony's voice—a sincerity, an openness—that she'd never known in him before. "Okay, Tony," she said after a few seconds, "just for a few minutes."

An hour and a half later Amber and Tony sat alone in the family room. Tony hurriedly wolfed down a slice of pie Amber's mother had forced on him.

"You know me pretty well, Amber, especially the wild side," he began, struggling to find the words he wanted. "I've been thinking the last few days about some of the things I've done. There are some things I'm not very proud of, especially when I hurt other people. I think what I did at the campout was wrong, and I've been wanting to say I'm sorry about it."

Amber could tell from his nervous fidgeting that Tony was agonizing through his apology. He was so skilled and confident in many areas that Amber had to appreciate his grit to follow through in an area where he was unsure of himself.

"Thanks, Tony. I'm all right now," she said guardedly.

"There's something else I want to say. I know you pretty well too—at least I think I do. You've avoided me since the campout, and I don't blame you. But I can tell that you've changed. I know you've been in church all your life, but I also saw what you used to do on Friday and Saturday nights. I was there, remember?

"But ever since the campout you've completely dropped out of the party scene. And now I see you hanging out with those Christian kids at school; you never did that before. What's going on with you?"

Amber hoped her suddenly accelerated heartbeat didn't sound as loud to Tony as it did to her. She'd heard of opportunities to witness being miraculously plopped in Christians' laps, but she never expected it to happen to her.

She wasn't sure about Tony's motive for asking. Maybe he was just trying to soften her up, hoping he could finish what he started at the campout. But being a charter member of the Liberation Commandos she knew she had to give him a straight answer.

"I've rediscovered God's love and forgiveness, Tony. I'm trusting His Spirit to lead and direct my life now." Amber felt proud that her spur-of-the-moment answer had been so straightforward.

But to Tony, Amber's response couldn't have been more confusing if she had delivered it in Swahili. "What?" he said, looking very puzzled. "You're trusting some spirit? Are you into one of those cult things?"

"No, Tony, I mean Christ is the center of my life now. I'm serious about my Christian life."

"My uncle talks a lot about being centered. He wears a crystal and goes to the New Age church that meets in the theater on Sunday mornings. Is that what you're into?"

Amber suddenly felt like she had just walked into her history class and then discovered it was exam day and that she had forgotten to prepare. *He doesn't have a clue about what I'm saying. How do I explain what's happened to me?* she thought desperately.

For the next fifteen minutes Amber did just what she would have done during a surprise history exam: She tried to snow her way through. She talked about Christ and Paul and the Bible and the Antichrist and Daniel in the lions' den—anything she could remember from Sunday school lessons and sermons she'd heard. Tony kept asking sincere questions, but Amber's answers just made him shake his head in confusion.

Finally he stood up to leave. "I don't know, Amber. I'm glad you've found something you can believe in. But it sounds too complicated for me. Anyway, thanks for letting me come over and apologize. See you at the game on Saturday." Then he left.

Amber sat in the family room alone for several minutes feeling her stomach knot up. *Way to go, Miss Liberation Commando,* she chided herself. *All that praying yesterday for kids to become Christians and you can't even tell Tony what one is.* She decided to call Duane or Liz in the morning and ask them what's so good about the good news when it's so hard to understand and explain. And she was sure she wanted the Commandos to talk about it next Thursday. In the meantime she headed to her room to call her friend Will.

The Inside Story: Telling the Gospel Truth

Remember: There are two parts to an effective strategy for introducing your non-Christian friends to Christ. Prayer is primary and indispensable. Without prayer you will be ineffective. But prayer isn't enough. At some point every student who doesn't know Christ needs to hear and understand the truth about what it means to be a Christian and to be challenged to trust Christ with his or her life.

If you were in Amber's shoes, how would you explain your Christian experience to someone like Tony? More specifically, if one of the friends or acquaintances you're praying for asked what it means to be a Christian, what would you say to persuade him or her to trust Christ?

What we're talking about here is the presentation of the gospel. *Gospel* literally means "good news." The gospel includes the good news of what God has done to provide forgiveness for our sin and the invitation to claim God's gift by turning from self and trusting Christ. You can pray for your friends until you're hoarse, but you'd better not, because eventually you're going to need your voice to share the gospel with them. If the people you're praying for don't hear the good news and respond to it by trusting Christ, they can't become Christians.

The gospel is the greatest news of all time, and piles of books have been written on the subject. But relax: You don't need to know every little detail about Jesus Christ and salvation in order to share the gospel with your friends. But you should have a good grasp on the basics, both for your own benefit and as a foundation for learning how to share the good news with others. Then as you grow in your walk with Christ you will become even more confident in sharing Christ with others.

A POSITIVE MESSAGE

Some of your friends may be like a lot of people today who picture God as some kind of celestial bogeyman. They may think God is just waiting for them to do something wrong so He can stomp on them and make their lives miserable. Or they may think God is out to trap them, trick them, hurt them, use them, or make fun of them.

But that's not the God of the good news. The heart of the good news is God's love. He loves us so much that He provided everything we need to know Him and experience eternal life (John 3:16). He's not plotting and scheming to make us miserable. Rather, God says: "'For I know the plans I have for you,' declares the LORD, 'plans to prosper you and not to harm you, plans to give you hope and a future'" (Jeremiah 29:11). And Christ said: "I have come that they may have life, and have it to the full" (John 10:10); "Peace I leave with you; my peace I give you" (John 14:27).

If you hope to persuade your non-Christian friends to trust Christ, you must first assure them that God is a loving God who wants to fill their lives with good things.

A SERIOUS PROBLEM

But there's something standing between your friends and God's love. It's called sin. Sin is the condition we were all in before we trusted Christ (Romans 3:23). As we discussed in Chapter 3, sin is basically an attitude of independence from God. It doesn't matter if your friends are violently anti-God or just indifferent toward Him. Their independent attitudes and actions keep them from knowing God and experiencing His great love.

God can't stand to be around sin (Psalm 5:4). As a result, sin separates the sinner from the righteous, loving God. Think about it: God loves us and created us to have a personal relationship with Him and experience His love. But our independence has cut us off from all God wants to do in our lives. Talk about a tragedy!

But wait; it gets worse. Since your unbelieving friends are cut off from the God who made them and loves them, their lives are totally controlled by themselves and their circumstances. They may think they're independent, but they're not. And as a result, they find themselves in a serious mess. They are really slaves to their own sinful nature (John 8:34; Romans 6:16). They are sitting ducks for Satan's destructive intentions (John 10:10). Ultimately, the consequence is eternal separation from God (Romans 6:23).

Your unbelieving friends may be prompted to do very good things (like saving the environment, doing charity work, etc.) or very bad things (like taking drugs, breaking the law, etc.) to try to soothe the emptiness they feel. But they are powerless to bridge the gap (Romans 5:6). They may not want to admit that they have a problem with sin; sin isn't a very popular topic these days. But unless they understand the serious nature of their sin, they will never understand why Christ died on the cross. And without an understanding of Christ's death and resurrection, they have no reason to trust Him with their lives.

THE PERFECT SOLUTION

Here's where the good news of God's love gets even better. While we were still blinded by Satan, trapped in darkness, and separated from God because of our unforgiven sin, Jesus Christ stepped forward and paid the penalty for our sin. He bridged the gap between us and God (Romans 5:8; 1 Timothy 2:5).

Remember Duane's story of the judge who paid the fine for his daughter's speeding ticket? God, the righteous, loving judge, saw that, in light of our sin problem, we had no way of paying the penalty ourselves. The price is eternal death! So He stepped down from the bench in the person of His Son, Jesus Christ, and paid the penalty for us. Then He rose from the dead, proving that His payment for our sin was acceptable to God the Father, guaranteeing us eternal life, and making it possible for Him to live in us by His Spirit. That is how we experience the fulfilling, powerful life He planned for us in the first place (1 Corinthians 15:3–5).

As you can see, the very center of God's solution to our sin problem is the death, burial, and resurrection of Jesus Christ. Without this, there is no good news.

Your unbelieving friends may believe the common myth that there are many ways to God, including living a clean life (as clean as possible anyway), obeying the Ten Commandments (at least most of the time), or being a very religious person (Christian, Buddhist, Muslim, Mormon—it doesn't really matter). But the Bible clearly states that Jesus is the *only* solution God has provided (John 14:6). Your friends must be brought face to face with this vital truth or their sin problem will never be solved.

A CRITICAL RESPONSE

As fantastic as it is, the gospel really won't be good news to your friends until they respond to it. The gospel is both the information about God's provision in Christ and an invitation to your friends to trust Christ by faith and welcome Him as their Savior and Lord.

The apostle John explained why he wrote down his account in a Gospel: "But these [facts about Christ] are written," he said, "that you may believe that Jesus is the Christ, the Son of God, and that by believing you may have life in his name" (John 20:31). As we tell others the good news, our presentation only becomes complete when we ask our friends to admit their need for Christ's forgiveness, turn from trusting themselves, other people, drugs, etc., and trust or believe in Christ.

"To all who received him," John 1:12 states, "to those who believed in his name, he gave the right to become children of God." Paul wrote in Ephesians 2:8: "For it is by grace you have been saved, through faith." And Jesus says, in Revelation 3:20: "I stand at the door and knock. If anyone hears my voice and opens the door, I will come in and eat with him, and he with me." Do you see the response required in all these verses? Your friends won't become Christians simply by osmosis, by hearing the good news of what God has provided in Christ or by being around you. They must respond by trusting their lives to Him. If you're not ready to ask them to make a decision, you're not fully prepared to share the good news.

Remember: Our responsibility is to tell or explain the gospel and invite people to respond. We cannot, however, control how people will respond. That is why we must share Christ by trusting the Holy Spirit to use us and then leave the results to Him. He is the One who takes our words and uses them to convict and convince individuals of their need for Christ.

When you get right down to it, the gospel is rather simple and clear. But in order to be prepared to share the gospel so your friends can respond and trust Christ, you may need some basic training. Amber's frustrating experience with Tony on Thanksgiving Day is about to bring this fact to the attention of the corps of Liberation Commandos of Eisenhower High School.

9

More Than Just Friends

Will almost didn't make it to the Commandos meeting on the first Thursday night in December. His mother picked him up right after school so they could drive out to a tree farm near Gilligan's Lake and cut down their Christmas tree. Dorina liked to decorate the tree early and enjoy it all through the month. Starting the Christmas celebration early was fine with Will too. He enjoyed the special togetherness Christmas brought into their relationship.

But Will, who since mid-November was the proud possessor of a learner's permit, had a little problem driving down the hill in the cold drizzle. Having piloted everything from biplanes to F-18 Hornets on his Mac, Will was a tad overconfident behind the wheel of his mother's sporty hatchback. He took a curve a little wide, overcorrected, and slid the rear wheels into a shallow roadside ditch. Neither the car, its occupants, their spirits, nor the six-foot Scotch pine lashed to the roof were injured. But it took an hour and a half for the tow truck to arrive and get them back on the road.

When Will got to the Cunninghams', Darcelle, Buster, and Joy already occupied the couch. Jason, in his customary fatigues, was draped over the old leather reclining chair. So Will took a place on the floor next to Amber, secretly content that he had the best seat in the house.

Before the meeting officially started, the group buzzed about last Sunday's surprise in church. The pastor had announced their efforts as one of the congregation's special prayer subjects.

"You know," said Will, "I thought of asking for the church to pray for us once, but, I don't know, I guess I forgot."

"Well," said Darcelle, "several adults from church have already called me to say they're praying for us. Neat, isn't it?"

Reggie and Krystal arrived then, explaining that they were late because of football practice. The Generals had made it to the state championship game this coming Saturday, which meant the team was practicing late every night. Everybody cheered Reggie and wished him well as the only Liberation Commando on the team.

Most of the sharing time was taken up by Amber relating her encounter with Tony Ortiz on Thanksgiving. The Commandos were fascinated as she told the story and explained her frustration.

As she talked, Will remembered hearing about it the first time when she called him. It was a conversation he would never forget. Amber sounded so helpless and dependent, and Will felt so protective. He realized something as he consoled her and prayed with her that day—not a conscious, logical realization but kind of a subconscious sense. His crush was "growing up." He honestly appreciated his friendship with Amber as much as he admired her silky black hair, shining eyes, and warm voice.

Will's expectations were maturing also. If somebody asked him, "Will you be Amber's lifelong friend even if she never thinks of you as a boyfriend?" he would have responded with a hesitant yes. But if he were asked, "Do you think her friendship can grow into romantic feelings for you just as your crush has grown into a deeper friendship with her?" he would throw a confident fist in the air and exult, "Yes!"

After Amber shared, Duane began his talk. "I really believe that Tony's visit with Amber last week is an answer to the prayer walk you guys did. I mean, can you think of anyone less likely to apologize than the state's best football player?" The group chuckled knowingly, and Jason added a genuine but rather exaggerated, "Praise the Lord!"

"It's great when somebody like Tony shows an interest in spiritual things. And Amber has a valid concern about how to share the gospel in a clear, simple way in those situations. But before we talk about a step-by-step gospel presentation, let's talk about the kids we've been praying for who aren't showing an interest yet. I've learned some things at the construction site where I work about building bridges of communication with non-Christians in order to share the gospel with them. The majority of the people we're praying for won't come to us as Tony did. So we have to go to them. I'd like to share with you some guidelines for building bridges to people."

Duane led the group into a Bible study on the whys and hows of building bridges of communication to non-Christian friends and family members. Will listened intently because he, like the other Commandos, had been praying for a short list of names. None of them had shown any interest in God yet, let alone shown interest in Will.

Will had added Tony to his list rather reluctantly after God challenged him at the football game to do something about Tony. *But what can I do?* Will had argued with God more than once since then. *Tony's a senior, and I'm a lowly sophomore. He plays football, and I fly 747s to O'Hare. How can I reach out to him?*

But Will's reluctance ran even deeper than the obvious lack of common ground between him and Tony. Will didn't want to admit it to himself, but he was afraid if Tony became a Christian, Amber's affections for him might rekindle. He could almost hear Tony's testimony: "I want to thank the Lord for my friend, Will McConnell, who shared the gospel with me and allowed me to finally get together with Amber Lockwood." The thought made Will cringe inside.

But as Duane talked, Will sensed that God was pushing Tony higher on his prayer list. Will couldn't explain it if he had to, even to himself, but he was becoming convinced that God wanted him somehow to reach out to Tony. As the Bible study continued Will quietly confessed his selfishness and resigned himself to do whatever God directed him to do.

There was another name on Will's prayer list that was climbing even faster than Tony's. Duane was not just talking about sharing the gospel with friends. He specifically mentioned family members. Will bristled inside at the realization that he had not included on his list the name that should be at the top: Roger Vickers—Will's father.

Nefarius hadn't been the same in the days since the explosion bounced him around the cave like a ping-pong ball. He stumbled glassy-eyed through the cave, babbling nonsense in his resonant, gargly voice while a couple dozen runts attempted a major overhaul on his PIT.

Maledictus had also come out of the experience a little the worse for wear. The lumps raised along his python body from the falling conduits left him looking like he had eaten several of the larger maintenance runts for dinner. But his most serious wound was internal, and he tried his best to keep it covered from his underlings. He had never experienced such a clash between his hatred and his terror for the Enemy in all his existence. What was worse, for the first time the terror seemed to have the upper hand. He had marshaled all his resources against the prayer walk and had lost. Two of the four units in the cave were in shambles. Maledictus found himself doubting the capability of his hardware and his staff to sustain the next clash. He feared that the brigadiers were massed at the gates.

As the runts scurried throughout the cave completing their repairs, Maledictus gathered Ratsbane, Stygios, and Nefarius in a corner. The sector boss tried to appear confident by keeping his swan head high, but his charges weren't impressed.

"I have applied for special assistance for this subsector," he announced loudly to be heard above the gargling Nefarius and the din caused by the runts in the cave.

"To whom have you applied, Maledictus?" Ratsbane pressed, implying in his tone, "and what good will it do anyway?" The events of recent months had increased Ratsbane's sense of hopelessness in the battle against the Enemy.

The swan-python's response provoked a disbelieving gasp from Ratsbane and Stygios and even shut up Nefarius: "Our plight has been reported to Central Command, and they share our concern. I have been invited to the Grand Chamber. I have been granted an audience with the Prince of Darkness himself."

As usual, the Commandos broke into their prayer groups at the close of Duane's talk. Duane challenged them to identify two or three people to whom they felt God was calling to establish a bridge of care and communication for sharing Christ. Amber named three girls on the rally team, and Jason identified two kids in his drama class. Then they turned to Will.

"I have so little in common with the two names at the top of my list," he said somewhat reluctantly. "I don't see how I can get close enough to them to share the gospel."

"Do you think God can find a way for you to get close to them?" Amber asked with a mischievous twinkle.

Will smiled and nodded. "You're right, of course—Ephesians 3:20, exceedingly abundantly according to His power working in me." Then he explained how Tony Ortiz got on his list.

"I'm really glad to hear that, Will," Amber said, sounding relieved. "I want Tony to trust Christ, but I don't think I'm the one to share with him. It's not because I blew it talking to him the other night. There are just some things between us that make it best for me to stand back."

Will didn't know if he would ever be able to tell Amber how well he understood. Then Will told his friends that his father was the other name on his list.

"I hardly know anything about your dad," Amber said with genuine concern. "All I know is that your parents were divorced a long time ago."

Jason and Will exchanged knowing glances. "It's a long story, Amber, and we'd better get some praying done," Will said, averting his eyes. He was warmed by her interest, and he really wanted to include Amber in this area of his life. But not yet. Amber read his body language and backed off respectfully.

The three of them joined hands and prayed conversationally for each other and for the persons they had mentioned. Amber prayed sweetly and insightfully for Will and "Mr. Vickers." Will had never felt so honored by a friend as in the words Amber used to ask God to help him build a loving relationship with his father. He couldn't keep a small tear from trickling down one of his cheeks.

When Will said the final amen, Jason jumped up to help Liz carry a platter of cookies and a pitcher of hot cocoa to the coffee table. Amber realized that Will was still holding her hand and staring at her. "Thanks for praying for me and my dad; it means a lot to me," Will said, still a little choked up.

Amber studied the face of her friend. His expression of appreciation was mixed with a flush of boyish embarrassment from holding her hand. She read the familiar kindness and interest in his eyes. Then she noticed for the first time how angular and manly his face was becoming. Amber was suddenly aware that Will wasn't just a good friend who happened to be a guy. Will was a nice-looking guy—a guy she'd never noticed this way before—who happened to be a very good friend. The realization almost caused her to jerk her hand away in embarrassment, but she didn't.

"Would you like to ride with me—well, with me and my mom—to the game Saturday?" Will felt such a rush from what he'd just done that he almost couldn't breathe.

"I can't, Will," she answered. "The rally team has to ride over on the team bus."

Will nodded, then lowered his eyes to cover his disappointment. "Oh, yeah, the team bus. I understand."

"But I could ride home with you." When Will looked up, Amber was smiling.

That's when Will received his first kiss—from Jason Withers. When Jason saw Will and Amber still holding hands, he couldn't allow the tender moment to go unnoticed by the rest of the Commandos. He sneaked up behind Will and planted a big, noisy kiss on his cheek. Will and Amber turned crimson, and the place went crazy with laughter.

The Inside Story:
Building Bridges
to People

Having launched a sustained prayer offensive for their friends and family members in darkness, the Liberation Commandos of Eisenhower High School begin to prepare for their one-on-one rescue operation. What about you? Are you praying for a list of people who need to trust Christ? Are you ready to take some positive steps toward sharing the gospel with them?

Maybe you're champing at the bit to get started. You're ready to start wearing your witnessing t-shirts (you know, like the one that says "Turn or Burn") to school instead of only to youth group. You want to pass out tracts at the local mall and put fish symbols on your book bag. And your life's goal is to be on television holding one of those John 3:16 banners at the Super Bowl.

There may be nothing wrong with any of these witnessing strategies. But if you want to be effective in sharing the gospel with friends and family members, there are some relational and communication skills you should practice. Remember: God will use you to share His message with people you know well, with casual acquaintances, and sometimes even with strangers. In the next few moments let's focus on those people you already know well and see often.

WHY BUILD BRIDGES?

There are many good reasons for building bridges of communication with people who don't know Christ.

1. You are filled to serve people. When God fills you with His Holy Spirit, He reproduces His supernatural qualities in you—such as love, joy, peace, patience, kindness, goodness, faithfulness, gentleness, and self-control (Galatians 5:22–23). But He didn't fill you with all this good fruit only to satisfy *you.* He also invests these qualities in you to equip you to get along with and minister to people. God is so intent on using you to relate to and serve others that He provides all the qualities you need to do so.

2. God planted you among unbelievers. If God's only purpose for your existence was to save you, He would have jerked you out of the world the moment you trusted Christ. And if He wanted you to spend your life only with other believers, you'd find Bible verses instructing Christians to run away from the world and live together in isolation. But after you trusted Christ, God left you right where you were—in the middle of a school full of non-Christians. He has planted you there so you can influence them and direct them to a personal relationship with Christ.

Unfortunately, Christians often tend to drift to one of two extremes in their relationships with non-Christians. Some think they're supposed to keep plenty of distance between themselves and non-Christians; others go to the opposite extreme by living just like non-Christians. But both of these extremes work against God's purposes. God has left you in the world, but you are not part of the world's system of values (John 17:14–15). As many have said, we are to hate sin but love the sinner. God has equipped you to build positive relationships with non-Christians without "defiling" yourself and without behaving as they behave.

3. Your unbelieving friends really desire to know God. They may not act like it most of the time, but your non-Christian friends have an inner desire to know their Maker. God installed that desire in their hearts when He created them. Many of their self-destructive activities are frantic attempts to fill their inner emptiness. As you get to know your friends better, you will see the inner needs they have.

HOW TO BE A BRIDGE BUILDER

Here are several practical steps for building bridges of communication with unbelievers in preparation for sharing the gospel with them.

1. Meet them on their turf. Friends do things together. You need to invade the territory of your non-Christian friends, learn what they like to do and go where they like to go.

If a friend is into tennis, develop an interest in tennis. This doesn't mean you have to become a tennis pro. Just show an interest in your friend's tennis, even if it's only to watch him or her play. Similarly, if she's into sewing or shopping, suggest doing these activities together. Get involved in your friend's interests as much as possible without sacrificing your personal standards (for example, "I'll go to the basketball game with you, but I won't go out drinking with you afterward").

Be a true friend to the unbelievers in your world. Be available when they need you. Sacrifice your time and energy to serve them.

2. Arouse spiritual curiosity. Your attitude, actions, and conversation will communicate to your non-Christian friends, "I have found something you really want and need." The way you handle conflicts with parents and friends, the way you respond to problems with grades and teachers, and the way you defuse pressure to join your non-Christian friends in doing something wrong will cause them to wonder what's different about you. You can only arouse curiosity in this way, of course, if you are walking in the Spirit on a daily basis.

Another way to stir up curiosity is by asking thought-provoking, open-ended questions. For example, ask "What do you think happens after you die?" "What do you think God is like?" "What's your greatest fear?" Make sure your questions focus on your friends' thoughts and feelings. Then listen to them carefully. If you show interest in what they think and feel—without judging them—they will listen when you share Christ with them.

3. Pray for opportunities and confidence to share Christ. Remember, just being a friend to some unbelievers won't make them Christians. They need to understand the gospel and respond to it personally by trusting Christ. Your constant prayer should be, "Lord, prepare my friends' hearts to hear and respond to the gospel. Give me Your strength and confidence to share with them."

Your friends may or may not give you a perfect opportunity to talk about Christ. If they do, that's great. But it's more likely that you will have to begin the conversation by asking if you can share something personal about your relationship with God. You may say, "Do you ever think about God? I do. I think about Him a lot."

Don't be mistaken: Your ultimate goal in your relationships with non-Christians is to share Christ with them and persuade them to trust Him as Savior and Lord. You may be friends with someone only a few days or weeks before you are able to communicate the gospel to him or her. Remain faithful in your friendship and patiently trust the Holy Spirit to help you know when to speak.

WHEN YOU SHARE YOUR FAITH

Remember these helpful tips when sharing your faith:

1. *Step into the opportunity confidently.* Don't be embarrassed or afraid. God has prepared you and your friends for this moment. Your friends need what you have to share. After they trust Christ, they will thank you for allowing God to use you in their lives.

2. *Be friendly but firm.* Don't turn into a fire-breathing preacher. These are your friends, remember? You're sharing what Christ has done in your life and explaining what He can do in their lives. By the same token, tell it the way it is. Don't soft-pedal the gospel so as not to offend your friends. They need to know the truth so they can be set free (John 8:32).

3. *Talk their language.* Avoid the temptation to switch into Christian jargon as you explain the gospel to your friends. Your church friends may understand words like *justification, sanctification, born again,* and *redeemed.* But your non-Christian friends may not have a clue about what these

terms mean. Translate the gospel into the language your friends understand without losing anything in the translation.

4. Use a simple step-by-step approach. How much of the gospel do your friends need to know before they can make an intelligent decision to trust Christ? Not very much, since the gospel is basically quite simple. There are several good, concise ways to present the basic gospel message and call for a response. One of them is the booklet, "Would You Like to Know God Personally?" which is reproduced in the Appendix. In Chapter 10 you will learn how to use this simple, effective tool to share the gospel with your friends. It's the tool the Liberation Commandos are practicing right now.

10

Bombs Away!

Will thought it was ironic that the Eisenhower Generals were getting bombed in the state championship game on Pearl Harbor Day, December 7. Late in the third quarter the Roseburg Bulldogs had a 33–9 lead. Tony Ortiz, Ike's all-state running back, had fumbled twice in the subfreezing weather and had been held to only thirty-five yards by Roseburg's swarming defense.

Will, Buster Todd, and Darcelle Davis were huddled together under an old quilt in the confetti-strewn student section agonizing through the massacre. As bummed as Will was over the game, he was warmed inside at the prospect of being with Amber after the game. His mother, who was sitting with a group of other parents, teased him about this being his first date. But Will insisted that he was only driving Amber home and that it wasn't a date with his mother along.

When Will wasn't watching Amber on the sidelines, he was looking for Tony or Reggie on the field. Will knew it was a humbling experience for Tony to be stymied in front of his family, friends, and several college scouts who had come to watch him. But Will admired him for fighting for yardage down after down. *I can't see how you're going to do it, Lord,* Will prayed silently as he watched Tony trot back to the huddle. *But if you can use me to reach Tony, I'm available.*

In the middle of a half-hearted Eisenhower spell-out, Will felt what he thought was a handful of cigarettes bounce off the hood and shoulders of his coat. He picked one of them off the quilt. It was a tightly rolled cylinder of paper—about the size of a cigarette—wrapped in red cellophane with the ends tucked in.

Will unwrapped the cylinder and unrolled the paper. It was a tract, the personal testimony of Teddy "Horse Face" Tyler, pro football player and outspoken Christian. Will looked around to see several distracted fans unrolling the brightly colored cylinders. A few kids were actually reading the story of Horse Face's conversion.

There's only one person I know who is crazy enough to throw "gospel bombs" at the state championship football game, Will thought. He turned around and scanned the crowd above him. Sure enough, the culprit was sitting on the top row looking as innocent as a cherub. Will scampered up the stairs and sat down beside the cherub before he could think about getting away.

"What's this all about?" Will asked, waving the tract under Jason's nose. Will was half amused at Jason's ingenuity and half ticked at the mess he had made in the stands.

"How did you know it was me, man?" Jason had that hand-in-the-cookie-jar look. He was wearing his ratty bombardier's jacket with a canvas flyer's cap pulled down over his ears and dark goggles over his eyes.

"Who else could it be, bud?" Will said, grinning. "Your imagination is in a class by itself. When you die, your brain will be on display at the Smithsonian."

"I did it because Duane has been talking to us about sharing the gospel at Ike," Jason explained, still smiling at the backhanded compliment from his friend. "I just thought I'd get a head start by carpet bombing the crowd with the Teddy Tyler story. People at a football game should identify with Horse Face, don't you think?"

"I think your enthusiasm is great, but I think Duane had more in mind. We'll find out Thurs—" Will was drowned out by a roar from the crowd as Tony Ortiz blasted through the line for a gritty fifteen-yard gain. The air around the two boys was filled with red and white confetti.

Duane did have something more in mind. The next Thursday night he distributed copies of the booklet, "Would You Like to Know God Personally?" to the Liberation Commandos. He explained that he and Liz had been part of a campus outreach group at college. They were trained to share their testimonies and present the gospel one-on-one using the booklet. Duane assured the group that there were many good tools available to present the gospel. But since he was familiar and comfortable with this booklet he had decided to train the group to use the same approach.

Some of the Commandos had seen the booklet before, but none had ever used it to lead someone to Christ. So Duane and Liz spent the two Thursday nights before Christmas teaching them how to prepare and share their testimonies and use the booklet to lead their friends to Christ.

On the second night Duane announced, "Now that you understand how to use the booklet, we're going to break into pairs and practice on each other." Everybody groaned good-naturedly. Then Amber and Krystal, Joy and Darcelle, Jason and Buster, and Will and Reggie pulled out their booklets and faced each other in pairs.

Each Commando had at least two turns presenting the gospel to his or her partner—except for Buster Todd. Buster's partner Jason was really into his role as a non-Christian. He kept distracting Buster by asking questions like, "But where did Cain get his wife?" or bragging about his life of sin and crime. At last Buster grabbed Jason playfully and wrestled him to the floor. "You'd better quit stalling and trust Christ," he threatened, "or I'm going to stuff this booklet up your nose." Jason's antics prompted Duane to share with the group some ways to respond to serious objections when making a gospel presentation.

The Commandos spent more time praying together that night than ever before. Despite the laughs that Jason had injected into the training sessions, the group was sobered by the realization that God was set to launch them into the one-on-one phase of their rescue mission at Ike. They prayed for each other and for their lists of names. At the close of their prayer time, Will slipped one of the booklets into his wallet. *I don't know if I'm ready, Lord, but I'm willing to be used*, he offered silently. Little did he know that God would take him up on his offer in less than forty-eight hours.

☆   ☆   ☆

"I still have some Christmas shopping to do," Amber told Will after the meeting as they slurped Coke floats. "Do you want to go to the mall Saturday? My dad will drop us off and pick us up."

"That's perfect!" Will answered. "I need to get my mom's gift, and she's in Phoenix again this weekend." Will was glowing inside. He couldn't think of a better way to spend the Saturday before Christmas.

Westcastle Mall was jammed, and after an hour Will was feeling like a fly speck again. Amber was constantly running into her friends from school. She warmly introduced Will to all of them, but then he stood at her heel like an obedient Labrador retriever while she socialized. Finally, Will excused himself to go into the bookstore to buy the world atlas Dorina wanted. Amber said she'd meet him at the food park in an hour after she looked at some girl things with Hillary and Lisa from the rally team.

Will found the atlas immediately. Then after fifteen minutes of browsing the computer section he turned to head

for the counter, almost running into another young cus-
tomer.

"Hello, Will." Will did a startled double take. He couldn't
believe it. The boy he'd almost run into was Marlon Trask.
Will and Marlon shared a Mac in their computer science
class. Marlon was one of three names from that class on
Will's prayer list.

Marlon was one of the geekiest-looking sophomores at
Ike. He was short and chunky, and his clothes always looked
about three fads behind the times. He didn't socialize well.
But he was sharp in programming, and he'd always been a
helpful partner to Will. Will didn't exactly like Marlon, but
he appreciated him and was concerned about him, especially
since God encouraged him to put Marlon on his prayer list.

"Hi, Marlon," Will said in a genuinely friendly tone.
"Doing some last-minute shopping?"

"Naw, I'm just killing time." Marlon explained in detail
what he'd been doing in the mall for the past four hours.

Will looked like he was listening, but his mind was
spinning in another direction. *He's on my list, Lord. Am I
supposed to share the gospel with him right here, right now?* Will
flashed on several reasons not to share: his inadequacy, his
fear, Amber returning and interrupting. But running into
Marlon in the mall like this was too bizarre to ignore. Will
decided to test the waters. "Would you like to go get a Coke?"

Marlon was obviously pleased at the invitation. "Yeah,
Will. That'd be cool." Five minutes later they were sitting at
a small table in the middle of the noisy food park next to
Santa's Workshop.

After a few minutes of small talk, Will bravely took a
shot at turning the conversation toward God as he had been
trained. "Marlon, this being Christmas and all, do you ever
think about spiritual things like God and heaven and stuff?"

Marlon's face darkened slightly at the question. "Not
much. My parents dragged me to Sunday school when I was
little. That's when my real dad was alive. My stepdad watches

sports on Sunday mornings. So I usually sleep in or work on the computer game I'm inventing."

Will's heart was racing. He sighed a silent prayer and said, "Yeah, God didn't used to be very important to me either. I've gone to church most of my life, more out of a sense of ritual than out of a relationship with God. But something happened at the end of the summer this year that changed all that and changed me. Can I tell you about it?"

Marlon looked more curious than skeptical and he nodded.

Will briefly told about the campout and Duane's challenge at the video party. "So just before school started I opened my life to God's love and forgiveness like never before. Celebrating Christ's birthday this year is something special to me because I'm learning to make Him the center of my life."

Will paused to see how Marlon was handling his presentation. He just sat there. Since Marlon wasn't running for the exit, Will swallowed hard and continued. "Speaking of Christ, Marlon, if you died today, do you know for sure that you would go to heaven?"

"What? Today?" Marlon pondered aloud. "How should I know?"

"Would you like to know for sure?"

"Well . . . yeah. Who wouldn't?"

Will took the booklet out of his wallet and began the presentation just as he had practiced it with Reggie Spencer. He read and explained about God's love, the problem of sin, God's solution, and the importance of trusting Christ personally. Will was amazed at how easily his words flowed and how attentive Marlon was. A shiver raced up his spine as he realized that God was actually leading him in his first real rescue operation.

"Is there any reason why you wouldn't want to trust Christ as your personal Savior and Lord right now, Marlon?" Will concluded.

Marlon looked away and shifted uncomfortably, say-ing nothing. Will knew that a battle was raging, and he silently claimed God's power to break the chains that held Marlon in darkness. Marlon turned back abruptly. "No reason. I'm ready." Will could hardly believe his ears as he listened to Marlon quietly pray to trust Christ. He couldn't see the brilliant blue-white cylinder around Marlon or the horrified demons fleeing for cover in a dark and distant place.

Marlon hadn't been gone more than three minutes when Amber hurried into the food park and found Will alone at the table. "I'm sorry I'm late, but you won't believe what happened!" she sang excitedly. "I was able to share the gospel with Hillary and Lisa, and Hillary prayed to trust Christ in front of Penney's!"

Will laughed out loud as his excitement over Marlon suddenly doubled. "While you were sharing with Hillary and Lisa, I was sharing with Marlon Trask. And he prayed to trust Christ right here at this table!"

All at once, Will realized he was hugging Amber in joyful celebration, and she was hugging him back. But he was even more shocked that the electricity that shot through him from being in Amber's arms couldn't match his elation at being used by God in the liberation of Marlon Trask.

The Inside Story: Sharing the Truth Step by Step

Think about the elements that combined to result in Marlon and Hillary's praying to trust Christ in Westcastle Mall.

First, there's the commitment of Will and Amber. They have been learning to walk in the Spirit and have made themselves available to be used by God in His rescue mission.

Second, there's prayer. Will and Amber have been assaulting the kingdom of darkness with prayer on a daily basis so that Satan's hold on Marlon and Hillary would be broken. Their consistent prayers were being answered.

Third, there's the servant's attitude they had toward their friends. Will related to Marlon mainly in their computer class. They aren't close friends, but at least Will shows an interest in Marlon through the common ground of mutual computer interests. Amber and Hillary are on the rally team together and are casual friends outside their rally activities.

Fourth, there's a tool—a simple, step-by-step method of presenting the gospel message. In this case, Will and Amber shared a brief testimony and then talked through the "Would You Like to Know God Personally?" booklet with Marlon and Hillary.

Most people have no trouble with the first three elements, but some hesitate at using a tool. They don't think a tool is very spiritual. But methods are neither spiritual nor unspiritual; they're just tools. It's the spiritual condition of the person using the tool that determines if it will be spiritually effective. If the tool is simple enough, it can be tailored to fit a wide variety of people with a wide variety of experiences, problems, and needs.

As Duane told the Liberation Commandos, there are a number of good methods available today for presenting the gospel simply and clearly. The method presented in this chapter is one of the most successful. If you're more comfortable with another approach, great! Use it. But if you're like most Christians, you're about as prepared to share a simple presentation of the gospel as Amber was when Tony came to see her on Thanksgiving Day. To be an effective commando in God's liberation army, you need to learn, practice, and use a simple gospel presentation method such as the one described in the following pages.

TELLING YOUR OWN STORY

At some point in your presentation of the gospel you should briefly tell the story of your relationship with Christ. In our story, Will compared his life as a nominal, church-going Christian to his vital walk with Christ. Think through your story ahead of time and summarize it in a few sentences that you can commit to memory.

There are three parts to an effective testimony.

1. Before trusting Christ. In a sentence or two, describe your life before you trusted Christ as Savior. What was the focus of your life? How did you try to find happiness and security? For example, Reggie Spencer might say: "I used to live on the wild side. I thought the thrills of sports, booze, and girls would keep me happy."

If you have been a Christian since childhood, describe your life before you yielded control of your life to Christ. Amber's comment might be, "Growing up in church, I thought the real fun things in life were the ones my parents said were wrong. I couldn't wait to try some of them."

2. How it happened. Briefly tell the circumstances that led you to trust Christ as Savior. When did you first understand the gospel? What made you decide to trust Christ? Reggie would probably say: "I heard a story about a judge who paid the fine for his daughter's speeding ticket. When I heard that, I realized what Jesus did on the cross. When I learned that God loved me enough to pay the price for my sin, I asked Him into my life."

3. After trusting Christ. Describe the difference Christ has made in your life since you trusted Him. What does Christ mean to you now? What changes has He made in your life? You might hear Amber say, "My life isn't perfect, but God has brought me to realize that He uses my parents to protect me from bad choices and hurtful consequences. That's made a big difference in our relationship."

As you prepare your testimony, tell it like it is. Don't jazz up the facts or glorify your past just to make your story sound more exciting. Also, avoid Christian jargon that non-Christians won't understand. And keep the focus on your personal relationship with Christ, not your church or organization.

Here's a challenge. Take a sheet of paper right now and write the first draft of your testimony in no more than eight sentences. Share it with a Christian friend and have him or her suggest how you could make it clearer and more relevant.

PRESENTING THE GOSPEL CLEARLY

(*Note:* Refer to a copy of the booklet "Would You Like to Know God Personally?" as you study this section. If you don't have a copy of the booklet, see the Appendix.)

One of the best ways to introduce a booklet presentation is by asking questions that arouse interest in spiritual matters. Will asked Marlon: "Do you ever think about spiritual things like God and heaven and stuff?" and "If you died today, are you sure you would go to heaven?" Other questions you may ask are:

- Do you think it's possible to know God in a personal way?

- How would you describe your relationship with God?

- Do you know what it means to be a Christian?

- The spiritual dimension of life has become very important to me. May I share with you what I've discovered?

- Recently I've been learning how to share my faith. Would you help me by giving me your opinion of this booklet?

Then ask your friends if you can read through the booklet with them. Follow these simple steps as you make your presentation.

1. *Read through the booklet aloud.* Hold the booklet so that both of you can see it. Then carefully and thoughtfully read through the entire booklet aloud page by page as your friend follows along. You may want to use your index finger as a pointer on each page so your friend is both hearing you read and seeing the words and diagrams.

2. *Personalize the message wherever possible.* The booklet can be read straight through without additional comments. But your goal is to help your friends understand these spiritual truths so they will trust Christ personally. So you may want to modify your reading by adding your own comments and personal examples where they are appropriate.

3. *Defer questions whenever possible.* Your friends may have questions about the message in the booklet. Be sensitive to their needs. If the question is appropriate to where you are in the presentation, you may want to respond right away. If the question is valid but off the point, ask your friends to save it until you finish going through the booklet. Their questions may be answered as you do so. If not, you can discuss it afterward.

4. *Invite a response.* At the conclusion of the presentation the booklet displays two circles, one picturing the self-directed life and the other the Christ-directed life. As you ask the two circle questions, be sure to wait for your friends to respond. If they indicate an interest in the Christ-directed life, follow up by asking if they are ready to trust Christ. Again, wait for a response. If the response is positive, ask them to pray and express their trust in Christ. The prayer in the booklet is very helpful because it suggests words they can use to express the desire of their heart to God. Then conclude the presentation by reading the rest of the booklet.

If your friends do not express an interest in the Christ-directed life or praying to trust Christ, don't be discouraged. Give them the booklet and encourage them to read it again and consider praying to trust Christ alone. Keep praying for your friends, and plan to meet them again and offer another opportunity to trust Christ.

DEALING WITH QUESTIONS

Your friends may have some questions or objections during (or after) the gospel presentation. Some questions are sincere and reflect legitimate concerns and needs. Other questions are insincere; they are asked just to stall you or get you off the point because God's truth is convicting them. Still other questions are asked to test your sincerity.

The most important aspect to consider in responding to questions of any kind is your attitude. Here are a few important guidelines to help you respond to questions positively.

1. Be as ready as you can be. Peter instructed: "Always be prepared to give an answer to everyone who asks you to give the reason for the hope that you have" (1 Peter 3:15). This doesn't mean you need a doctorate in biblical studies before God can use you to present the gospel and answer questions effectively. It just means you should be constantly learning and preparing yourself to respond to others. When your non-Christian friends ask questions you can't answer, write them down and go search for answers. Ask your parents, pastor, or youth leader to help you when you get stumped. Books can also help. You may want to look at *Don't Check Your Brains at the Door.* See the section of Additional Resources at the back of this book.

2. Don't feel threatened; be confident. Paul wrote: "I am not ashamed of the gospel, because it is the power of God for the salvation of everyone who believes" (Romans 1:16). When you are presenting the gospel, you don't need to feel ashamed, embarrassed, or threatened. You are Christ's ambassador, and when you discuss the gospel with your friends, God's power is at work in you. Be confident without being pushy or proud.

3. Don't argue. You will never be able to argue someone into trusting Christ. God's Word commands us not even to try (2 Timothy 2:23–26). Simply share the gospel with your friends in the power of the Holy Spirit. Your loving attitude will be your most persuasive argument.

4. Answer questions honestly. If your friends ask tough questions, don't try to snow them to make yourself look good. It's okay to say, "Good question. I don't know the answer, but I'll be happy to do some research on it and let you know what I discover the next time we meet."

Some of the Liberation Commandos are experiencing the excitement of sharing the gospel with their friends and seeing them liberated from the kingdom of darkness. Now they need to see how their new skills fit into an overall liberation strategy for Eisenhower High School. So during a New Year's Eve getaway they began to discuss a plan for the rest of the school year. Meanwhile, another high-level (or should we say low-level?) strategy session was being conducted in the smoky chambers of the Prince of Darkness himself.

11

Gully-Washer

It was almost midnight. Half the Commandos were asleep as Duane steered the church van up the mountain road toward the cabin where they would enjoy a New Year's getaway before school started again. Will was crammed in the back corner of the crowded van, and his buns ached from sitting for so long. But he didn't really mind the discomfort because Amber was crammed in next to him.

It had been the best Christmas Will could remember, even better than the year he got his Mac. For openers, he'd never been so content in his relationship with God. He knew Christ was alive within him. The Christmas carols had more meaning this year as Will realized that he was right in the middle of what the infant Jesus had come into the world to do.

Then there was Marlon Trask. Will still couldn't get over the awesome experience of leading Marlon to Christ that Saturday before Christmas. At Duane's suggestion, Will had met with Marlon a couple of times over Christmas break to encourage him in his new Christian life. Amber had done the same with Hillary Putnam. Now Marlon and Hillary were the newest Liberation Commandos, and they were crammed into the van with the rest of the group.

And then there was Amber. This was no blazing love affair, Will realized. After all, they had only held hands three or four times, hugged only once—more from joy than from passion—and never come close to a kiss. But Will was certain that Amber's interest in him had grown beyond the brother-sister stage of a month ago. Will had given his feelings about Amber to God and was content to let their relationship develop at His pace. Yet he still couldn't believe that a girl this beautiful and popular was dozing on his shoulder.

Only one shadow darkened Will's best Christmas ever, and that shadow belonged to Roger Vickers. Will had been praying for his dad, but rather half-heartedly because he seemed so distant, so unreal, almost like a fictional character he'd only read about. His dad had sent him another turkey of a Christmas present—a gigantic chemistry set—and a Ziggy card simply signed, "Your Father." Will sent back a religious card inviting him to come visit, but he wasn't sure he meant it. Will knew his dad needed Christ, and he was pretty sure God wanted to use him somehow to share the gospel with his dad. But Will was having a hard time believing it could happen.

The Commandos spent New Year's Eve day inner-tubing on the snowy slopes around the cabin and pelting each other with snowballs. Then after a great lasagna dinner they gathered in front of a crackling fire in the stone fireplace to welcome the new year with popcorn, marshmallows, Oreos, and Cokes.

Duane thought it would be a good idea to share some of the highlights of the year. Nobody was surprised that most of the comments related to what God had been doing in the group since the campout at Gilligan's Lake. Marlon and Hillary took it all in with wide-eyed wonder.

As usual, Joy Akiyama was one of the last to speak. Joy had been especially quiet during the getaway. Her startling story revealed why.

"Most of you know I'm adopted, but no one except Darcelle and Liz knows that I was severely slapped and spanked almost every day by my adoptive parents. And on many nights my father came into my bedroom and . . ." Joy couldn't bring herself to finish the description, but she didn't have to.

"For most of my childhood I believed that all children were treated like I was. But now I understand that I was physically and sexually abused by my parents. I've had this anger boiling inside me all these years. Even when I became a Christian I kept hating them, but I said nothing to them or to God about it.

"But since I have been making Christ the focus of my life, I've been talking and praying with Liz and Darcelle about how to deal with my past. Recently I realized that I had to confront my parents and forgive them for hurting me." She paused a moment to choke off a tear. "So on Christmas Day that's what I did."

Joy couldn't hold back the tears any longer. Darcelle and Liz surrounded her with tissues and hugs while the rest of the Commandos sat sniffling and praying. When Joy regained control of herself, she told how angry her parents were that she would speak of such things. They showed no remorse and refused to accept Joy's forgiveness, saying they did the best they could as parents. Joy closed by asking the Commandos to pray that God would give her an opportunity to share the gospel with her parents.

The group gathered around Joy and prayed for several minutes. But Will was having a hard time thinking about Joy. Her revelation hit him hard. He realized that he had been carrying a truckload of conflicting feelings about his own dad. He felt abandoned and unloved. He felt ashamed about being an illegitimate son and even more ashamed that he couldn't admit it to anyone except Jason. And yet he loved his father and wanted to share the gospel with him. Being stuck in the middle of his unconfessed feelings was suddenly very painful.

After Duane closed the prayer time for Joy, Will spoke up. "Before we get out of the praying mood, I have a couple of needs I'd like you to remember in prayer." Will held himself together as his confession tumbled out. But when the group huddled around him and began to pray, the dam holding his feelings in check crumbled and the tears came like a flood. Jason prayed for Mr. Vickers to get saved. Amber and Darcelle asked God to mend the hurt in Will's heart. Everybody chipped in a sentence or two, including Marlon Trask, whose prayer was a masterpiece of childlike simplicity. Will filled tissue after tissue as he felt a gigantic weight being lifted from his shoulders.

After praying for Will, each of the Commandos, including Duane and Liz, took a turn in the middle of the circle and was lifted to God by the others. It turned out to be one of those gully-washer prayer times that sometimes happen when people are transparent before God and their brothers and sisters in Christ.

The prayer meeting ended just in time for the Commandos to salute the new year with whoops, high fives, hugs, and a rhythm band of pots, pans, and spoons. After twenty minutes of noisy celebration, Duane asked everybody to gather by the fireplace again before turning in for the night.

"Last year, as Liberation Commandos we steadily bombed Satan's strongholds with our prayers. And we equipped ourselves with a tool to reach out to the captives and liberate them from the darkness. Marlon and Hillary are proof that the liberation of Eisenhower High School has begun." The group cheered wildly, and the two newest Commandos grinned with appreciation.

"But if we're going to make a significant impact on the campus for Christ this year," he continued, "we must have a battle plan. We need to lock on to a number of specific target groups and pray for them. We need to plan strategies to reach these kids, disciple them, and train them to be disciplers. In short, we have a lot of work to do. We've only just begun to fight."

Jason jumped to his feet and lifted his nearly empty Coke can. "I propose a toast." The rest of the Commandos eagerly grabbed their drinks and stood. "To a year of liberation," Jason said.

"To a year of liberation," the Commandos chanted in unison. Then they lifted their Cokes to the Great Liberator and drank.

Ratsbane didn't really like the idea of accompanying Maledictus to Satan's Grand Chamber. He reasoned that the problem in Subsector 477 was not the best grounds for a visit. The Prince of Demons had been known to vaporize mutants on the spot and recycle them as runts for less consequential blunders. But Ratsbane's objections only infuriated his sector boss. So he reluctantly waddled alongside the slithering swan-python through the endless network of bustling tunnels leading to the Grand Chamber.

The closer they came to Central Command the less crowded the passageways appeared. Few mutants traveled in this direction on purpose, and those who wandered into the Prince's labyrinth of private tunnels without carrying an official medallion were subject to the whims of the chamber guards. Satan was served by some of the largest, most grotesque mutants Ratsbane had ever seen. His twitching eye became more exaggerated with every sentry they passed.

At last Maledictus and Ratsbane reached the outer court of the Grand Chamber. It was filled with swirling, noxious smoke. And it vibrated with the roar of nearby flames. As the pair ascended the broad stairway leading to the Grand

Chamber, the medallion dangling from Maledictus' swan neck was inspected repeatedly by fearsome guards. Finally they reached the summit and stepped through a massive stone arch.

Ratsbane had heard that Satan employed a number of gruesome appearances, so he didn't know what to expect. When his eyes focused on the monstrous form hunched across the dim chamber, he began to tremble so violently that he could no longer feel his eye twitch.

The Great Satan sprang fully upright on his hind legs and glared down at his visitors. For this occasion he was transformed into a towering, fire-breathing tyrannosaur. Ratsbane and Maledictus nearly fainted at the sight.

"Which one of you is Maledictus of Subsector 477?" His voice roared like a furnace, and flames lapped at his spiked teeth as he spoke.

"I am, your majes—" Maledictus' response was cut short by a bolt of flame spat from the tyrannosaur's mouth into the swan-python's open beak. The bolt jerked Maledictus off the floor, uncoiled him straight as a board with a loud zap and blew the end of his tail clean off. Ratsbane tumbled backward and watched in horror as the skewer of flame slowly rotisserized Maledictus in mid-air. In seconds he was barbecued from the inside out, splattering the floor below with sizzling chunks of python flesh. In seconds Maledictus' steaming parts were in a wheelbarrow headed for the recycling cavern.

"Demon Ratsbane, you're now in charge of Subsector 477," the tyrannosaur flamed. "Get back to your post and stop those rebels. And you'd better hope you never see me again."

Ratsbane scrambled to his feet, skittered down the stairs and disappeared into the tunnel, cursing all the way.

☆   ☆   ☆

The Liberation Commandos spent their Thursday nights in January discussing and praying about their strategy. They agreed that a divide-and-conquer approach was the most efficient. Each member would target a group of non-Christians at Ike and focus on praying for them and getting to know them better. They would plan some kind of activity for their target groups to occur around Easter. Then they would especially pray and plan to use these events to share the gospel with their respective target groups.

At the last meeting in January, the Commandos gathered at the Cunninghams' to reveal their outreach strategies to each other.

"My drama class is presenting *Harvey* in the spring," Jason reported. "Buster and I both have parts in the play. After the performances we're going to invite the cast to Buster's house to see the classic *Harvey* video starring Jimmy Stewart. Then we'll share our testimonies and present the gospel."

Amber spoke next. "Hillary and I have targeted the rally. On Easter weekend we're having a sleepover with the girls. We'll give our testimonies and show a neat video my cousin sent me."

Joy and Darcelle had targeted the school newspaper staff. Reggie and Krystal felt a special tug toward several of their friends in the wild bunch. Duane was going to work closely with them to plan an outreach event for that group.

Will spoke last. "Marlon and I have been meeting together a couple times a week for Bible study and prayer. We've been praying about sharing Christ with our computer science class. I'm going to be in two computer classes this spring; in one of them I'll be the teacher's assistant. We're going to have a pizza party for both classes at my place the night before Easter."

At the close of the meeting the Commandos renewed their commitment to pray for each other and for the continuing liberation of their non-Christian friends at Ike.

Despite Will's clear focus on reaching out to his computer classes, he was still perplexed about Tony Ortiz. He
prayed for Tony every day, but they still had no common
ground. Will doubted that Tony even remembered his name.
On the first day of the spring semester, his doubts became
reality.

Will stood at the back of the basic computing class
welcoming a line of freshmen and sophomores and directing
them to their workstations. Suddenly he was face to face with
a tall, muscular senior wearing a letterman's jacket and a
look of mild disgust.

"Tony, what are you doing here?" Will asked in disbe-
lief. "This is basic computing. You must be in the wrong
room."

"I'm in the right room, Willie," Tony said dejectedly. "I
failed this class as a sophomore. I've got to pass it this
semester or I don't graduate."

Will tried to keep a grin from arousing Tony's suspi-
cion. "Tony, my name is Will, not Willie. I'm the T.A. in this
class. Maybe I can help you pass it this time."

Tony studied Will for a few seconds. "Maybe you can,
Will."

The Inside Story:
Following the
Battle Plan

Someone once said, "If you aim at nothing, you'll surely
hit it." Similarly, when you think about liberating your non-
Christian friends from their captivity to sin and Satan, if you
don't define your target and plan how to reach it, you won't
be very successful.

In 1 Corinthians 9:24–27, the apostle Paul compares the Christian life to the attitude of a runner training for a race. Paul has two things clearly in mind.

First, he challenges us: "Run in such a way as to get the prize" (verse 24). Evangelism isn't a fun run; we're going for the gold. We're out to rescue as many people as possible—and as soon as possible—to the glory of God. We must give it all we've got.

Second, since he's so determined to be a winner, Paul states: "I do not run like a man running aimlessly" (verse 26). If you're going to compete in a race, you must be well trained. But if you hope to win, you must also have your goal clearly in view and follow a carefully planned strategy. To maximize your effectiveness in your evangelizing, you need a strategy for reaching and discipling your family, school, and community.

Here are several principles that will help you and your group determine an effective strategy for evangelizing your world.

ENLARGE YOUR VISION

Many Christians are ineffective in their efforts to reach others because they don't have a true picture of what God is able to do. They look at many of the unbelievers in school or in their community and say, "I can never reach him," or "She wouldn't be interested in the gospel," or "He would laugh in my face if I shared my testimony with him." They forget that not only does a PowerLink exist between the praying believer and the prayer-answering God, but another PowerLink connects the witnessing believer to a listening friend. God's power *surges* through both links!

Ephesians 3:20 challenges us to define our vision for evangelism based on what God can do through us, not on what we can do in our own strength and ability: "Now to him who is able to do immeasurably more than all we ask or imagine, according to his power that is at work within us." Sit down with your own group of Liberation Commandos and brainstorm what you would like to see happen on your campus. For example, ask yourselves questions like these: Who would we share Christ with if we knew they wouldn't reject us or Jesus Christ? Of all the people we know, who is the person least likely to ever become a Christian?

When defining your vision, don't just talk about things you think you can do. That's too narrow a vision. Discuss the "immeasurably more than all we ask or imagine" things you would like to see the Lord do through you.

MOBILIZE YOUR SUPPORT

You may wonder why someone like the apostle Paul was so successful in the ministry of evangelism. One reason is the prayer support he sought from other Christians. For example:

- To the Ephesian believers he wrote: "Pray also for me, that whenever I open my mouth, words may be given me so that I will fearlessly make known the mystery of the gospel" (Ephesians 6:19).

- To the Roman church he wrote: "I urge you, brothers, . . . to join me in my struggle by praying to God for me" (Romans 15:30).

- To the Colossian Christians he wrote: "Pray for us, too, that God may open a door for our message, so that we may proclaim the mystery of Christ" (Colossians 4:3).

- In his second letter to the Thessalonians he wrote: "Finally, brothers, pray for us that the message of the Lord may spread rapidly and be honored, just as it was with you" (2 Thessalonians 3:1).

Paul was an effective Liberation Commando because he mobilized an army of prayer warriors who covered him as he battled on the front lines. You need the same kind of support. Ask your parents, your pastor, your youth leader, your Sunday school teacher, and your Christian friends to pray for you as you share the gospel. Report to them regularly on how God is answering their prayers.

Another reason Paul was so successful was the inner circle of co-laborers who served with him. As you watch Paul operate in the Acts you don't see him flying solo. He had Barnabas, Silas, Timothy, Priscilla, Aquila, Apollos, and numbers of other men and women he recruited to work alongside him.

In our story, Will and Marlon are co-laborers in reaching the computer classes. Amber and Hillary are a team, as are Darcelle and Joy, and Reggie, Krystal, and Duane. As you identify the non-Christians God is calling you to reach, try to find at least one other person who will join you in reaching that target. Evangelistic partnerships and teams are vital for prayer and accountability.

FOCUS ON YOUR WORLD

When you start thinking about how many unbelievers need to be evangelized in your school, you could easily get discouraged by the enormity of the task. It's good to pray for your whole school. But you need to begin your efforts on your group of friends, your classes, or your sports teams. From that inner circle you can work outward, praying for, targeting, and sharing the gospel with other groups. Use the following steps to help you identify your world and plan a strategy to reach it.

1. Define your target. Take a blank sheet of paper and draw a simple target with a bull's eye in the center and two other circles around it. In the outer circle write the names of a few groups you are in contact with on a regular basis (band, 4-H Club, student council, algebra class, rally team, basketball team). Why focus on groups you're already in? Many of these kids are already your friends, and the gospel spreads fastest among friends. Also, when these people trust Christ, you already have a relationship in which you can disciple them.

In the next circle write the names of individual family members, neighbors, close friends, or coworkers who don't know Christ. These are the people you spend most of your time with. It's only natural that you would want to share the gospel with those closest to you.

In the bull's-eye of the target, write the names of one or two groups and several individuals to whom you will commit yourself to share the gospel. Before you write these names, ask God to impress on you which names to write. Also, talk with other members of your discipleship group to make sure several targets are being covered. If other members of your group are targeting the school band you're in, you may want to focus on another target no one is covering.

2. Pray for your target. Remember: Prayer is the primary weapon in your spiritual arsenal for liberating captives from Satan's power. Keep the list of names where you will see it often (in your Bible or taped to your mirror, for example) and pray for these people daily.

3. Surround your target with love. Paul talked about becoming a servant to those he wanted to reach with the gospel (1 Corinthians 9:19–23). Build bridges of love and concern to your non-Christian targets by becoming their servants. Meet their needs for friendship by doing things with them and spending time with them. Offer to help them where you can.

4. Present the gospel to your target. Hopefully you have equipped yourself with a tool for presenting the gospel to others simply and clearly. Pray for, watch for, and create opportunities to share Christ and call for a commitment.

One effective strategy for presenting the gospel to a target group is to plan an outreach event (party, sleepover, dinner, etc.). During the course of the event, you and other Christians may share your testimonies, give a presentation of the gospel, and invite a response. If you're not reading this book as the companion to the "See You at the Party" video series, check it out. The video series builds to a specific outreach event. Look for the details at the back of this book.

5. Follow up those who trust Christ. Remember, your goal in sharing Christ is disciples. Your task of sharing the gospel with your non-Christian friends doesn't end when they trust Christ. They need to be discipled to become disciplers of others. Principles for follow-up and discipleship will be discussed in greater detail in chapters 13 and 14.

6. Allow the Holy Spirit to lead. It is important to pray, plan, and follow through as you share the gospel with your special target groups and individuals. But it is also important to stay closely tuned to the Holy Spirit in case He wants to change your plans and lead you in another direction (Acts 16:6–10).

What will happen when you and your group launch a prayerful strategy for reaching the people in your world? Only time will tell. The Liberation Commandos of Eisenhower High School are going to be shocked out of their socks by the results of their ministry. And the mutants of Subsector 477 are going to lose more than their socks in the process.

12

The Main Event

Ratsbane was numb with panic, and he couldn't get away from Satan's Grand Chamber fast enough. He waddled unsteadily through the tunnels leading back to Subsector 477, cursing in anger one moment and wailing in fear the next. He thought about going AWOL and hiding out in some remote, lower chamber of hell. But he knew Satan's goons would eventually find him, and he would end up on the tyrannosaur's flaming rotisserie like Maledictus and then be reconstituted as a lowly maintenance runt. His only chance for survival was to somehow smash the rebellion in Subsector 477. But what chance did he have?

Ratsbane had only traveled a mile or so through the sparsely populated tunnels when he realized he was being followed. The shuffling of many feet marching in unison behind him grew louder. He couldn't bring himself to turn around. He was sure that Satan had changed his mind and sent his goons after him. *This is it,* he whined to himself. *I'm dead meat.*

Ratsbane decided to go down fighting, so he whirled around with a hateful roar. But he saw nothing—that is, until he looked down. Stretched out before him down the tunnel was an army of runts, odd little bits of fur, feathers, scaly flesh, and mismatched limbs. Ratsbane thought there must be hundreds of them. They were toting spools of cable, stone conduits, panels, and tools. And the runt leading the parade, more fishlike than anything else, was carrying a large scroll.

"Why are you following me?" Ratsbane tried to sound ferocious, but the runts didn't even flinch.

"The Great Satan himself sent us," said the fishy-looking runt with the scroll. "We are at your command to remodel Subsector 477 for a major assault. Here are the plans, direct from the Grand Chamber."

Ratsbane eyed the runt suspiciously as he took the scroll and unrolled it. It was a blueprint. The detailed drawing showed the Prime-evil Impulse Transducers in Subsector 477 linked to at least fifty more PITs in the adjoining subsectors. The plans called for new access tunnels between the caves and a command center mounted on the tower where Ratsbane first met Maledictus. And inscribed across the sketch of the command center in Satan's own hand were two words: Foreman Ratsbane.

Ratsbane erupted with a shriek of joy and swelled with arrogant pride. He rerolled the scroll with a flourish and handed it back to the runt. *An invincible array of firepower designed and commissioned by the mighty Satan himself,* he thought haughtily, *and it is under my command. At last the rebels shall be vanquished, and I again will be commended.*

Ratsbane wheeled around and began traveling forward again, and the runt army obediently fell in behind him. The confident swagger quickly returned to Ratsbane's gait, and the tic in his eye disappeared. And with every step his hatred for the Enemy flamed hotter within him. "This will be a spring those Westcastle punks will *never* forget," he cackled wickedly.

☆   ☆   ☆

Will wondered how he would survive high school if every semester was as busy as this one. He had a full load of classes and piles of homework every night. In February, the Liberation Commandos began meeting on Monday and Thursday nights to study, pray, and encourage each other in their outreach endeavors. And every lunch hour Will was either praying with Amber and Jason, discipling Marlon, or eating lunch with three other guys from his computer science class who were on his prayer list.

Tony Ortiz had also landed on Will's weekly schedule. After Will refused to sell him answer sheets or doctor his grades in basic computing, he offered to tutor Tony on his own Mac one or two nights a week. For their first sessions together, Tony treated Will almost as impersonally as he did the Mac. But soon Will's attitude of helpfulness (well saturated with prayer) began to penetrate Tony's hard shell.

Will was also trying to save some time for his mother. They tried to have a cup of cocoa before bedtime and pray together, that is, when Dorina wasn't stuck in a late meeting or out of town. Will felt good that his father was becoming a regular topic of their conversations and prayers together, even though his mom still nursed some inner wounds from her relationship with Roger Vickers.

The relationships that seemed to suffer the most from Will's time crunch were the two most important to him. Although he and Amber spent a lot of time together in Commando activities, their busy schedules left little time for just the two of them. And Will's early morning quiet time with God sometimes turned into an unplanned nap after a late night of homework. But Will understood the power of prayer like never before in his life, so he prayed for his father, Tony, and his computer class buddies every morning, even if he had to skip breakfast to do it.

During March the Commandos' prayers focused sharply on the outreach events they had been planning for Easter week. Three of the activities—the rally team sleepover, the party for the *Harvey* cast, and Will and Marlon's pizza party for the computer classes—were all planned for Saturday night, Easter eve.

The weekend before the party, Will phoned each of the kids he and Marlon had targeted and invited them to the party—with one exception. Will was suddenly nervous about inviting Tony. This wasn't going to be a kegger with the wild bunch. This was a crowd of computer jockeys— wimps, dweebs, and geeks by Tony's standards—getting together for pizza, Cokes, computer games, and a presenta- tion of the gospel. Sure, he and Tony were friends now— just barely and only because Tony needed him. But every time Will screwed up his courage to pick up the phone, he quickly put it down again. *No way would he be interested in coming,* he argued with himself. So he never called.

But at the Thursday night meeting before the party, Duane's pep talk to the Commandos made Will realize he'd made a big mistake. "For several weeks now we've been praying and preparing to share the gospel and see captives liberated. Maybe you haven't seen much progress. You feel like you're trying to dig an escape tunnel for your non- Christian friends through a mountain with a pick and shovel. You're tired, you're discouraged, and you wonder if you'll ever reach the other side.

"What you don't realize is that God is tunneling through the mountain from the other side," Duane said. "And He's doing most of the digging. Don't give up on Him. Keep doing what He has given you to do. You never know when He's going to bust through from the other side and your friend will be free."

Will saw himself sitting dejectedly in a dark tunnel marked "Tony Ortiz." Duane was right. Will had forgotten that Tony's escape tunnel was mainly God's concern. All Will had to do was pray for him, love him, and seek to share the gospel with him. God would take care of the rest. Will didn't know if the pizza party was part of God's tunnel, but he knew he had to invite him.

"Hi Tony, this is Will." He fumbled with the phone cord nervously. "I've been meaning to tell you about a pizza party I'm having Saturday night at my place for some of the kids in the computer classes. I'd like you to come too."

There was a long pause on Tony's end. "Uh-h-h, a party? For the computer dudes? Are you kidding? I'm not really, er, I think I'm busy Saturday night. Yeah, I already have plans, Willie. Sorry."

Will hung up the phone. He was really confused. He had hoped God wanted Tony at his pizza party. But that was obviously the last place Tony wanted to be. Will quickly picked up the phone again. He had to talk this over with Amber.

☆ ☆ ☆

Ratsbane surveyed his new command center proudly. From his elevated command position he was on line with more than fifty PITs that had been crammed into the caverns around his tower. Bundles of cable linking the hardware carpeted the floor in every direction. The army of runts scurried busily through the complex like ants at a picnic. Dozens of surly mutants, imported from other divisions, had joined Nefarius at the controls of the newly installed apparatus. And Ratsbane's adjutant with the crooked pelican beak stood at his elbow.

"The refurbishing has been completed just in time, Foreman Ratsbane," Stygios reported guardedly. "The rebels are mounting a major offensive this weekend. Their concerted prayers have kept the runts hustling with repairs in all subsectors even during the installations. But the activities they've planned for tonight go beyond prayer. They intend to pummel our captives with large doses of their truth."

"Not to worry, Stygios," Ratsbane said confidently, scanning the bank of monitors that surrounded his command center. "They have yet to feel the sting of my new power. But the time has now come. I see that many of our captives are getting ready to attend the rebel functions. Stygios, alert all subsectors to flood those PIT lines with darkness and keep them from arriving. And commence the attack on the rebels leading the offensive. We'll hit them so hard that even the brigadiers won't be able to save them."

Stygios obediently sounded the alert and repeated Ratsbane's orders. Immediately the steady hum from the caverns around the tower escalated into a grinding howl as the large fleet of PITs fired salvo after salvo into the conduits.

Ratsbane watched eagerly as some of the captives waffled about attending Jason's cast party, Amber's sleepover, and Will's pizza party. He watched round after round of tempting impulses buffet the Commandos. But they refused to buckle. Ratsbane saw Jason, Buster, Amber, Hillary, Will, and Marlon make last-minute preparations and kneel to pray. Soon most of the invited captives began streaming to the three homes. Ratsbane winced at the first round of muffled explosions and yelps of pain coming from the caverns as conduits and control panels began to spark, flame, and shatter.

"Hit them harder, Stygios," Ratsbane snapped. "These meetings must not succeed." Stygios relayed the orders. The roar from the laboring PITs intensified, and the explosions and agonizing cries from the caverns kept pace.

Ratsbane, Stygios, and the assault force of mutants held their own until the Commandos began sharing their testimonies and the gospel with the captives they had invited. Then the complex under Ratsbane's command started coming apart at the seams.

"Brigadier alert in 453!" Stygios screamed. Just then a

deafening concussion rocked the tower. Jagged pieces of mutant and machine blew out of the opening of subsector 453 in a cloud of blue-white smoke. Ratsbane yowled at the sight on the monitor of a brigadier enveloping a girl with whom Amber was sharing the truth of God's love and forgiveness.

"Unit 453 is destroyed and the cave has collapsed!" Stygios reported in panic. His statement was punctuated by two more thunderous booms. "And there go 468 and 459!" Ratsbane screamed a desperate order, but two more explosions drowned him out.

Within minutes, pandemonium reigned. The caverns around the tower began exploding and collapsing with the regularity of drum beats, spewing their mangled contents into the main cave surrounding Ratsbane's tower. Then the command center itself went off like a Roman candle. Bolts of blue-white light ricocheted off the walls, vaporizing everything they touched. Ratsbane dived under his console just as a bolt zapped near his antenna. The flash looped around Stygios like a noose and—*poof*—his pelican and beaver parts were rearranged as he staggered and fell against a piece of conduit.

Ratsbane stayed huddled, dazed, and trembling on the floor until the siege was over. Then he slowly stood to survey the damage. The cave around the tower was layered with thick smoke. Waves of debris and body parts had washed up the sides of the tower. Ratsbane was alone, and all was quiet except for a whish of static pouring from three monitors that had miraculously survived the destruction.

It was about midnight, and on one monitor Jason's cast party was breaking up. Jason and Buster were saying goodbye to their friends at the door. In Jason's hand were two cards given him by fellow cast members who indicated they had trusted Christ during their presentation.

☆   ☆   ☆

At the sleepover, several girls were in the family room watching videos. But Amber and Hillary were in another room praying with two girls who had trusted Christ.

Will and Marlon had invited more than twenty guys from their computer class. Three had shown up.

"What are we going to do with all this extra pizza?" Will whined when their guests had gone. They had ordered pizza for fifteen, figuring that not everyone would show. They had not been prepared for such dismal results.

Will had fumbled miserably through his testimony and a gospel presentation, and no one had responded. He tried not to reveal his dejection in front of Marlon. Afterward, they wrapped the surplus pizza for the freezer.

"Guess we blew it pretty good, huh, Marlon?" The two boys collapsed on the couch, staring at their feet, and feeling sorry for themselves. As they sat in silence, however, Will thought of calling Duane to pour out his disappointment. Finally, after much prompting by the Holy Spirit, he gave in, dialed the number and told Duane what had happened.

"I know you're disappointed, Will, but you have to remember two things," Duane said calmly. "Number one, your first time at doing *any*thing is bound to be less than perfect." Will wondered if Duane was thinking of his disastrous first attempt at water-skiing. "And number two, God doesn't call you to save people. That's His job. He calls you to share Christ with them and leave the results with Him. Did you share Christ with others tonight?"

"Well, yeah," Will answered.

"Then God is pleased. You were obedient in sharing the gospel. Tonight you sowed some seed. It may not spring up into a beanstalk overnight, but you've been faithful, and that pleases God. How about a word of prayer?"

Will's answer was interrupted by a knock at the front door.

"Hold on, Duane, somebody's at the door. Be right back."

Will opened the door.

"I was just on my way home from another party." It was Tony Ortiz. "I thought I'd stop in and see if there was any pizza left." Tony almost seemed embarrassed and unsure of himself, as if he'd just been caught cutting school.

"You bet, Tony. Come on in!" Will pulled out the pizza he'd just put away and popped a few slices into the microwave. As he came back to the living room, he saw the phone on the table and remembered he'd left Duane waiting.

"Uh, sorry Duane," he said as nonchalantly as he could. "Listen, Tony Ortiz just came by. I'll talk to you later, okay?"

"That's great, Will. I'll start praying for you as soon as I hang up."

Will dropped the phone into the cradle and snatched the pizza out of the microwave.

"So how was your other party?" he asked, as Tony nibbled at the edges of a hot slice of pepperoni and mushroom.

"Not so great. Actually, it was a lousy party. A couple of my friends got bombed, and they ganged up on me. So I left. I guess the guys I thought were my friends weren't really," he sighed.

Buoyed with courage and faith, Will boldly stepped into the opportunity at hand. "The main reason Marlon and I had the pizza party was to share with some of our friends something that's very important in our lives. Would you mind if I shared it with you?"

"I don't know why not," Tony answered.

Will and Marlon each shared a simple testimony just like they did at the party. Then Will pulled out a well-worn copy of the his booklet. He read through it page by page, and Tony looked on with interest.

Will was somewhat surprised when Tony indicated that his life was best represented by the picture of the self-directed life in the booklet. But Will held his breath as he asked, "Tony are you ready to trust Christ?" Tony said nothing as he stared transfixed at the booklet. The moment seemed an eternity to Will.

Suddenly Tony lifted his head and said coldly, "I've got to go!" Before Will could say a thing Tony was out the door. Stunned by Tony's quick departure, Will turned to Marlon, "What did I do wrong?" Will glanced at his watch. It was a little after 1:00 A.M. Easter Sunday morning.

Ratsbane danced in hellish glee as the bright glow of a brigadier darted off the monitor screen in retreat. "Increase the power! We can't lose this one to the enemy," roared Ratsbane. The main cave shook under a mighty surge of the Prime-evil Impulse Transducer.

"I don't know how long the PIT can hold out," shouted Stygios.

"I said *increase power* you dastardly dimwit," Ratsbane commanded. "We've got to have more power!"

The Inside Story: Reaching Out in a Big Way

As illustrated by the Liberation Commandos, outreach events may or may not bring immediate results. The key is to be faithful in presenting the gospel and leave the results to Christ. But remember a flashy, fun-filled outreach event is not a substitute for your everyday, personal, one-on-one witness.

You still have a responsibility to pray, build bridges, and share the gospel with your own non-Christian family members and friends, even when they don't respond positively.

The types and varieties of outreach activities you can use are virtually limitless. But there are some general guidelines that apply to nearly all of them. In this chapter we will cover these guidelines by answering three foundational questions about outreach activities.

WHAT IS AN OUTREACH ACTIVITY?

An outreach activity is a regular event designed to reach non-Christian friends. It is a party or activity in a comfortable, neutral environment, with the purpose of sharing the gospel in a positive way. Let's break that definition down into four parts.

1. Christians invite those who don't know Christ. The activity you plan should be something your friends enjoy doing. Remember, it's for them, not you. For example, you probably won't plan a Bible study for this activity, because most non-Christians don't appreciate the Bible and may feel out of place.

2. A party or activity. This activity should be social, that is, helping kids do fun things together, like a make-up party, a scavenger hunt, a board game party, a video party, a beach party, a cookout, or a costume party.

Your activity should be especially tailored to the group you are targeting. If you're inviting the football team, for example, a board game party probably wouldn't go over as well as a Frisbee golf tournament or a burger cookout.

One of the best ways to ensure fun and interaction is to serve food at your event. Whatever else you do, make sure you spice it up with pizza, burgers, sloppy joes, ice cream, or whatever gets the gastrointestinal juices flowing in your crowd.

3. A comfortable, neutral environment. Many times your non-Christian friends will feel uncomfortable attending a party at a church. They may put up their defenses before you have a chance to share your faith. So you may consider having your outreach activity somewhere other than the church. Stay in neutral territory, such as a home, a park, or a community center. As your friends feel more a part of the group, the transition will be made easier into the life of the church.

4. *Sharing the gospel in a positive way.* The ultimate goal of your activity is to present the message of Christ to your friends and give them an opportunity to trust Christ. Your presentation is important and should be built around a theme. We will expand on this idea in a moment.

WHAT ARE THE PIECES AND PARTS OF AN OUTREACH ACTIVITY?

1. *Social interaction.* The first part of your activity should focus on interaction and entertainment. This includes food. Refreshments can happen before, during, or after the event (or all three!). It doesn't have to be a full meal, but some kind of food and/or beverages should be served.

Someone should introduce the people responsible for the event, make everyone feel welcome and at ease and explain the purpose of the event. He or she may say, "We invited you here to have a good time. We also want to share with you something that has become very important to us and our faith in God."

Someone should be prepared to lead the group activity (game, skit, scavenger hunt, video). The activity should be broad enough to interest all your guests. This is an important time for getting to know each other better and helping everyone feel comfortable.

2. *The presentation.* After everyone has had a good time of fun and interaction, call them together for a time of discussion and your presentation. You can introduce the

subject of knowing God in a variety of ways: a speaker, videos, etc. You can begin by saying something like, "It sure is great having all of you here. I want to use this time together to share something very special I have learned about knowing God in a personal way. I think you will find it very interesting."

Have one or two students share their testimonies. Testimonies should be brief (three to four minutes), clear, and simple. They should avoid religious jargon and church preference. Keep the focus on Jesus Christ and what He means to you.

There are numerous ways to present the gospel to your non-Christian friends in a positive way. Plan your presentation around a theme. If you're having a make-up party for girls, for example, your theme could be attaining inner beauty or how Christ makes us attractive on the inside. If your party is for jocks, you can focus on being a real winner in life.

You can also show a film or video (sports videos of Christian athletes, a famous speaker, a or dramatic story). You can invite a guest speaker your friends would enjoy or make a live presentation yourself. Your presentation should be concise, simple, clear, illustrated (flip chart, etc.), and well practiced.

In most situations you will want to conclude the presentation by inviting people to pray a simple prayer to trust Christ. You can do this by asking those who want to trust Christ to pray silently a prayer you say aloud. This prayer time should be done clearly and carefully so everyone understands the opportunity they have to trust Christ. Ask everyone to bow their heads in respect for those who are ready to trust Christ at that moment.

After the presentation and the invitation to trust Christ, pass out blank cards and pencils and ask your guests to respond to the presentation. Ask them to include name, address, phone number, and their comments about the activity. Then ask them to place a check by their phone number if they prayed to trust Christ during the presentation. This will help you make a follow-up call or visit. We'll discuss follow-up in greater detail in Chapter 13.

3. Divide and Conquer. Perhaps the most effective way to maximize your impact is on a personal level. Break up after the speaker or video and talk one-on-one with the guests, preferably with the friend you yourself invited! This action immediately puts into practice all the training you received earlier.

You could make the transition by saying, "The speaker tonight talked about knowing Christ personally . . . have you ever heard that before?" Be sensitive to where he or she is at spiritually. Know that you may be simply cultivating the soil of his life by building a friendship. But if he is responsive, you should go on to sow the seed by injecting the gospel into that friendship (either through your personal testimony or reading the gospel booklet). Ask permission to share the "Would You Like to Know God Personally?" booklet, or some similar tool. As you talk you may find he is ready to trust Christ. Then it's time to reap by asking, "Is there any reason why you wouldn't trust in Jesus right now?" If you find he's ready, pray together right there in a corner of the room. Be sure to follow up in the next couple of days.

This personal presentation of the gospel sets an example for those responding to Christ. If a student receives Christ after talking with another student, the model of peer-evangelism is seen as being normal. If the student receives Christ at the invitation of a thirty-year-old speaker, he may conclude that until he's an older speaker, he's not obligated to share Christ. Begin immediately by showing that witnessing is a natural part of every Christian's life.

HOW DO WE PLAN AN OUTREACH ACTIVITY?

Here are the simple steps to guide you through the planning stage for a successful activity.

1. *Choose your activity.* Decide what your activity will be, but base it on the interests of your target group. Clearly define your purpose (what do we want to accomplish through this outreach?). List everything that needs to happen between now and the activity. Begin bathing it in prayer and do so throughout the planning process.

2. *Assign responsibilities.* Divide responsibilities equally. For example, if there are three of you planning the activity, split the duties into thirds. Make sure everyone knows exactly what responsibilities he or she has. Meet together often to compare notes and hold each other accountable.

3. *Invite and advertise.* Send fliers or invitations at least ten days prior to the activity. Call everyone a few days later to confirm the invitation and find out how many are planning to attend.

4. *Practice your presentations.* The individuals sharing their testimonies and presenting the gospel should practice them ahead of time for clarity, brevity, and simplicity.

5. *Gather all materials.* Think through the entire activity and list everything you will need to make it happen. For example: food, drinks, service items (plates, cups, napkins, forks), props for games or skits, flip chart for presenting the gospel, response cards and pencils, VCR and monitor (if needed). Gather the materials and get them to the site on time.

6. *Make a reminder call.* Call the invited guests the day before the activity to remind them about it and get a count of how many are planning to attend.

Will, Amber, Jason, and the other Liberation Commandos are ecstatic about what God did during their outreach events Easter week. But they're not ready to ride off into the sunset. Remember, the ultimate goal of evangelism is disciples. Their ministry of evangelism continues as they begin to disciple their friends who trusted Christ and keep on reaching out to those who need Him.

13

We've Just Begun to Fight

Jason Withers really outdid himself. He arrived at the Commandos' meeting the Monday night after Easter dressed as a sixteen-star general. His parade uniform was a collection of thrift store garments representing every branch of the armed forces. His gaudy ensemble of epaulets, stripes, buttons, and braids was topped off by an old Salvation Army hat with sixteen gold stars glued to the brim. The front of his olive drab coat was plastered with decorations—everything from authentic ribbons and medals to smiley face buttons and old Sunday school attendance pins.

The Commandos howled as Jason strutted around the Cunninghams' living room saluting everybody and acting like a pompous general. Then, in mock ceremony, he called each Commando to "ten-hut" and presented them with one of his decorations.

As the last of the decorated Commandos sat down, Jason took off his hat and spoke as himself. "While I still have the floor there's something else I'd like to say. We all know that we can't claim any credit for what has happened in our lives or for the liberation of our friends who trusted Christ last week." Several hummed their agreement. "So I'd like you to join me in a salute to our Commander-in-Chief for all He has done."

At first it seemed corny seeing Jason stand stiff as a flagpole with his head lifted toward heaven, his eyes closed, and his right arm holding a smart salute. But his friends soon caught the reverent spirit of his act. Silently, one by one, they stood—Will, Amber, Darcelle, Joy, Reggie, Krystal, Buster, Marlon, Hillary, Duane, and Liz—and joined Jason in his unique tribute to the Great Liberator. After several moments of silence, Will led the group in a prayer of thanks to which everyone added their whole-hearted amen.

"Thanks, Jason," Duane said as they were seated. "The laughs were great as always, and the salute was very appropriate. Now let's hear just exactly what did happen last week."

The next half-hour was riddled with exclamations like, "All right!" "Praise the Lord!" and "I can't believe it!" as the Commandos shared the results of their outreach activities. With a note of disappointment Will told how Tony had shown up after midnight and at least listened to a simple step-by-step gospel presentation. In all, ten students indicated that they had trusted Christ during the various events. The excited chatter grew louder as the Commandos began to discuss future outreach events in hopes that Tony and others would finally trust Christ.

"Wait a minute, wait a minute," Duane called out, waving his hands to quiet the group. "You can't just leave these new believers behind like trophies on a shelf while you go off to rescue others. The evangelism part of your responsibility for them has past, but the discipleship part is just beginning. Yes, there are a lot of students who still need to be reached. We need to keep praying for Tony and the others and sharing the gospel with them. But we also need to care for these baby Christians and help them grow in their new Christian faith."

The Commandos nodded knowingly, slightly embarrassed at their thoughtlessness. Duane had coached them since they became Commandos that reaching kids and discipling them were part of the same operation. Jason spoke for everyone when he said, "I guess we need to put away our parade uniforms and get back into our battle fatigues."

"That's right," Duane said. "We have invaded Satan's dominion and rescued some captives through prayer and sharing the gospel. And it's great to rejoice in that. But the devil doesn't give up even though he's been defeated. He's trying to deflect our attention from the importance of encouraging and nurturing these new Christians. And I'll bet he's already at work plotting to discourage these new Christians so they won't grow and reach others."

The main cave ceiling and command console of Subsector 477 was all but destroyed. A horde of maintenance runts were dispatched from the Grand Chamber to survey the damage.

"Mmm, one of the worst I've seen lately," said a maintenance runt as he picked at the wall of debris clogging the cave opening. "These rebels are really learning how to use their weapons."

"Don't speak of it, you fool!" Ratsbane lashed at the runt. "We must concentrate on reopening the cavern. We must resume the attack on these rebels before they reproduce again."

At Ratsbane's signal the runts surged forward and began to clear the devastation from the complex. Reusable PIT parts, of which there were only a few, were stacked along the tunnel walls. The maintenance runts shouted at each other as they went about their work.

In spite of the bickering and backbiting of the swarming company of runts, Subsector 477 was excavated and refitted in record time. New PIT consoles and monitors were installed, and shafts of stone conduit rose to connect the apparatus to the PIT lines above.

"There are two ways to derail the Westcastle rebellion, Stygios," Ratsbane said as the first bank of monitors blinked to life. "First, the seasoned rebels are vulnerable to pride and complacency over what they have accomplished. Flood those human tendencies with ME impulses. Tickle them with thoughts of having arrived spiritually. Tempt them to let down, relax, drop their guard. They'll stop praying soon about those they haven't reached, and they will be useless to the Enemy. Lukewarm rebels always contribute to our cause.

"Second, the newest rebels will shrivel up when they begin to doubt what happened to them. Pepper their minds with questions. Make them wonder if their experience was only a fleeting emotional high. If their minds are preoccupied with doubts, they won't be able to digest the Enemy's truth. Their growth will be stunted; they will end up spiritual retards. And a retarded rebel is almost as good as a captive to us."

Stygios snorted and giggled with anticipation as he punched in the coordinates for a young boy who was just waking up to the strains of a Wounded Twinkie song on his CD player.

Will rolled over in bed with a sleepy moan. The speakers on the shelf above his bed softly called to him. *Let me hold you, let me touch you, let me kiss you all through the night.* In his semi-consciousness Will realized that his Wounded Twinkie CD had been playing continuously as he slept. He hadn't listened to the Twinkie in months. But for some reason he slid the disc into his player late last night while doing homework, and then he fell asleep without turning it off.

Will knew it was time to get up and have devotions. Although he did occasionally miss his devotions, a definite habit had been forming since he became a Liberation Commando. His concern for Tony, his dad, and others had urged him out of the warm sheets morning after morning for Bible study and prayer. But he figured he had done his part and if they wanted to reject Christ it was their choice. Will's sense of urgency seemed suddenly dull. He snuggled under the covers to enjoy the warmth of his bed just a few minutes longer.

Somewhere in the twilight zone between being asleep and awake Will saw himself seated on the platform in the school auditorium before the entire student body. He knew he was there to make a gospel presentation to the audience. But he found himself enjoying the speeches of those introducing him. Marlon Trask stepped to the podium and praised Will lavishly for leading him to Christ. Jason stood up and roasted him with a few good-natured jokes. Duane Cunningham was next, saying that Will was the most mature Christian boy he'd ever met.

Just as Will stepped to the podium to speak the bell rang, and the crowd quickly filed out of the auditorium. He was a little disappointed that he couldn't give his presentation. But he felt real good about the nice things everybody said about him.

The auditorium finally emptied except for Will at the podium and a beautiful rally girl sitting in the front row smiling at him. Amber was dressed in a white pullover sweater with a block red E on the front and a short, red pleated skirt.

Somewhere a band began playing a Wounded Twinkie song. Amber stood up and started singing the words to Will: "Let me hold you, let me touch you, let me kiss you all through the night." As she sang she danced a sexy dance that made Will boil with desire. With her eyes fixed on Will and her arms outstretched, she began moving slowly up the platform stairs.

"No, no, no!" Will yelped as he flew out of bed, suddenly fully awake. He switched off the Twinkie, popped the CD out of the player, and Frisbeed it angrily across the room into his bookcase. "This is just what we were talking about last night," he muttered dejectedly. "Kick back for just a minute and the devil's there to pin you to the floor."

He rubbed his eyes and squinted at the clock. He should be heading out the door for school right now. He'd slept through devotions and breakfast. He started for his closet, then turned and dropped to his knees beside his bed. "Lord, I admit that I've taken my eyes off You and focused on myself the last couple of days. And I know the devil would like to plant new seeds of pride and lust in me and spoil the good things You have done. But right now I resist him in Your name and claim Your forgiveness. Help me encourage Marlon today and be a godly witness to Tony. Lord Jesus, continue to use me in Your rescue operation."

Will was dressed and out the door in five minutes. He wished he'd had more for breakfast than a toothbrush full of Crest.

Will's experience that morning made him more sensitive to Tony's need to know Christ and he wanted to talk to him. But Tony didn't show up for school the fourth day in a row.

That evening Will was dozing in front of the television in his living room. Suddenly he was jolted by a loud knock at the door. As Will opened the door Tony Ortiz darted past him without saying a word. Will followed him up the stairs to his bedroom. Both boys sat down and stared at each other. Tony broke the silence.

"Will, I don't know if I can explain what happened to me. It was that booklet—the prayer in that booklet—I couldn't get it out of my mind."

Will leaned forward in anticipation as Tony continued. "When I left your place I just kept driving. I went all the way to my cousin's place upstate. And on the way I kept praying that prayer from the booklet. I think I did it!"

Will read his indecision clearly. "Well, Tony, did you really mean it when you prayed and opened your life to Christ and trusted Him as your Savior?"

Tony paused as if counting votes. "Yeah, I really did."

Will's heart was pounding with excitement. His thoughts raced as he searched for his next question for Tony. *What do I say next? What am I supposed to say?* He thought. *Please Lord help me!* Then it came.

"Then where is Christ today, right now?" Will asked.

Again Tony paused to weigh his feelings against the facts. "I guess He's in my life." Will went on without hesitation.

"Remember Revelation 3:20?" he said as he tapped the reference into his computer's concordance. The verse flashed up on the monitor. "Read this part again."

Tony scooted closer to the screen. "'If anyone hears my voice and opens the door, I will come in.'"

"Did you open the door?" Will pressed.

"Yeah."

"Did Christ come in?"

"Yeah."

"Then, according to this verse, where is He now?"

Tony smiled and tapped his chest with his finger. "Right here."

"That's right, Tony. He's there because you trusted Him to forgive your sins and invited Him to come in—and He did. The devil will try to convince you that you're no different because you don't feel any different. Feelings come and go, but Jesus doesn't. He's there to stay."

Will didn't get much sleep that night, and neither did Tony. Will sensed the mighty PowerLink between himself and God's Spirit and how it was flowing from him to Tony. His bold approach opened the door to a flood of questions Tony was harboring. Will couldn't get over the transformation represented in Tony's immediate hunger and thirst for righteousness. The two boys talked well past midnight about God and the Bible and following Christ just like brothers.

☆   ☆   ☆

Ratsbane watched in helpless terror as a gloriously bright brigadier continued to dance the liberation dance around Tony Ortiz. As the last cylinder burst through Tony's PIT lines and he was completely set free, the newly refitted command console around Ratsbane suddenly disintegrated in a blinding, sizzling hail of sparks and flying stone. The main cave shook for only a few seconds before the ceiling split open and then collapsed with a horrendous roar. Ratsbane screamed to Stygios and Nefarius to call the maintenance runts immediately. Ratsbane reared back and roared a devilish oath that shook what remained of Subsector 477. "I will not be defeated," he screeched, "I will not be defeated!"

The Inside Story:
The Well-Grounded New Believer

When Satan fails in his attempt to discourage you or keep you from leading others to trust Christ, he doesn't trudge away whimpering in defeat. He regroups as quickly as possible and sets out to keep your new Christian friend from growing and maturing in his faith. This means that your friend needs encouragement and spiritual food as quickly as possible. If Satan can prompt you to think that the person you've brought to Christ doesn't need your attention, he has achieved a big part of his goal.

When you commit yourself to lead a person to Christ, you also commit yourself (or someone else) to follow him up and feed him spiritually. Delivering spiritual "children" has many similarities to delivering physical children. Newborn Christians need care.

Follow-up and discipleship are exciting and rewarding responsibilities. But as you boldly take steps to help new Christians grow, realize that you have no more ability to produce maturity in your Christian friend than you had to cause his spiritual birth. God brings the growth; you are His tool (2 Corinthians 3:4–6). You must ask God to give you His wisdom and ability to "parent" and serve the new Christian. Your friend needs you now as much as ever.

How do you follow up someone who has just received Christ? You have three distinct roles to play in his life: a parent, a teacher, and a friend.

PARENTING NEW CHRISTIANS

Have you ever noticed how helpless newborn babies are? About the only things they can do for themselves is breathe and mess their diapers. If newborns don't have someone to feed them and care for them twenty-four hours a day, they won't make it.

When new believers first trust Christ, they are new-borns inside. They were born into God's family, and they need the care and protection of a spiritual parent—especially in the first weeks and months of their Christian life. And if you are responsible for a person trusting Christ, it is natural that you fill the role of spiritual parent for this person (1 Thessalonians 2:8–12).

So what does a spiritual parent do?

1. Check vital signs. The first few days are critical for new Christians. They may be tempted to doubt that they are really different. The emotions they may have experienced when they trusted Christ may go away, making them wonder if Christ really came into their life.

It's important that you get together with new believers within a day or two to see how they are doing. Take the initiative by suggesting the time and place, but accommo-date yourself to their schedule. When you get together, focus your visit on them. Ask about their interests. Assure them that you care about them and their new life in Christ, and that you're available to talk whenever they need you.

2. Provide nourishment. Just as a baby needs food to survive, so a new Christian needs God's Word to begin mature growth. The Word says: "Like newborn babies, crave pure spiritual milk, so that by it you may grow up in your salvation" (1 Peter 2:2).

One of the first things new believers need is assurance about what happened to them when they trusted Christ. On your first visit together review the following basic facts about their new life in Christ:

- When you trusted Christ, you became a child of God (John 1:12).
- Your sins were forgiven (1 John 1:9).
- Jesus Christ is in your life (Revelation 3:20; John 1:12).
- He will never leave you (Hebrews 13:5–8).
- Your old life is gone. You are a new creation in Christ (2 Corinthians 5:17).
- You have received eternal life (John 5:24; 1 John 5:12–13).

3. Provide bonding relationships. It has been proven that newborn babies develop abnormally if they are not held and cuddled. Newborns must bond in their relationship with those who care for them.

New Christians also need to get in touch and involved with other believers. Introduce them to Christian friends and your leader or pastor right away. Invite them to church with you. Welcome them into your Bible study or prayer group. They need fellowship with good Christian friends to help them develop their faith.

TEACHING NEW CHRISTIANS

Fewer and fewer non-Christian kids today come from a religious background or understand the basics of what the

Bible teaches. One of the greatest needs of those who trust Christ is to be taught those basics.

You have the opportunity to serve those you bring to Christ as a teacher. In addition to the assurance your friends need from the Scriptures, there are many other things they need to learn about being a disciple of Christ. For example, they need to:

- understand the role of confession of sin and forgiveness in their daily life (Romans 5:6–9; 1 John 1:9).

- understand and experience the power they have through Christ's Spirit, the Holy Spirit, living in them (Romans 8:9; Ephesians 5:18).

- learn to pray and study the Bible on their own (2 Timothy 3:16–17; Philippians 4:6–7).

- understand the importance of becoming part of a local body of believers (Hebrews 10:25).

- learn how to share their faith with others (Romans 10:13–15).

One of the best ways to fulfill your role as a teacher is to meet with new Christians regularly for study, fellowship, and prayer. During your first follow-up visit, ask, "Do you want to grow as a Christian?" Your friends will undoubtedly answer yes. Then suggest that you meet together regularly for the purpose of study and growth.

If at all possible, invite your friends to be part of a small study and fellowship group with other young Christians. Get together personally or as a group at least once a week. If you miss a session, try to reschedule it within forty-eight hours instead of letting the week pass without meeting.

Four key elements should be included in your weekly meeting:

1. Sharing. When you meet, spend some time talking

about what's going on in your lives. Focus on what you see God doing and how you are growing in Him.

2. Study. Devote a significant portion of your time to Bible study. It is often helpful to work through a prepared study course together. Select something that will help them with their basic growth as a Christian. Encourage them to work through the lessons during the week so you can discuss their discoveries during your weekly meeting. One such study is the *So You . . .* series, by Chuck Klein. New Christians should begin with the book, *So You Want Solutions.* The series is available at your local Christian bookstore.

Your friends also need to learn to study the Bible on their own. Soon after you begin meeting regularly, share some simple guidelines for personal Bible study, such as the following:

- Spend fifteen to thirty minutes a day in Bible study. As you sit down to read, ask the Holy Spirit to help you understand what you study.

- Use a Bible translation you can understand. Start by studying the Book of Mark, John, or Romans.

- Keep a notebook and pencil close by for jotting notes (for each section you read, ask yourself: What is the main point of this section? What does it teach me about God, Jesus Christ, and the Holy Spirit? What does it teach me about myself? What am I going to do about what I learned?).

- Conclude by thanking God for what you learned. Ask Him for the confidence and power you need to apply His Word to your life.

3. Questions. Your friends may have many questions. Allow plenty of time for this in your meetings. Don't feel that you should be able to answer every question. It's okay to say,

"I don't know; let's find out together," or "I don't know, but I'll do some studying on it so we can talk about it next time."

4. Prayer. You have the opportunity to teach new Christians how to pray as you spend time praying together week by week. Emphasize that prayer is simply talking to God about your thoughts, feelings, and needs. Encourage simple, conversational prayer.

BEING A FRIEND TO NEW BELIEVERS

In addition to *parenting* and *teaching* a new Christian, the third vital role you can play in a new Christian's life is that of a friend. New Christians desperately need Christian friends immediately after they trust Christ. They may need to cut back on some of their activities with old friends because they are no longer in line with their new lifestyle.

Don't encourage your friends to abandon all their old friends; those are established relationships for sharing Christ. But offer yourself as a supportive, caring friend so they are not left to grow alone. Here are some suggestions for nurturing friendships:

1. Do things together. Relationships are built on time spent together. Attend Christian activities together (such as church, Christian campus groups, concerts). Do your homework together. Go shopping together. Work out together.

2. Be an encourager. Your new Christian friends may have some rough edges. They may struggle fitting into their new life in Christ. They may have old sins and habits to deal with. But suppress your desire to constantly correct or criticize them; be as positive and affirmative as you can. Expect the best from them, but focus on encouraging them where they are succeeding, not chipping at them for their weaknesses. Tell them personally about the positive things you see in them. Write notes of appreciation to them. Phone them occasionally to share a Scripture verse or just to say, "Hey, I'm thinking about you and praying for you."

3. *Be available.* Become a biblical servant to your friends (1 Peter 5:2–5). Put your friends ahead of yourself. Be there when they need you. Give of your time, effort, and possessions to serve them. Be ready to listen without giving advice. Your selfless availability and service communicates your acceptance of them.

The school year is nearly over. A lot has happened to the members of the Westcastle youth group since they first met at Gilligan's Lake. As they return to the lake for a Memorial Day picnic, they realize that their outreach efforts don't end with the school year . . . or ever. They have been called to be liberators for life.

14

A Day to Remember

Will didn't mind being a little late for the youth group's Memorial Day picnic at Gilligan's Lake. It was a good excuse to borrow his mom's car and exercise his new driver's license. And he looked forward to driving to the lake alone with Amber instead of being crammed into one of the church vans with the rest of the youth group.

As they drove toward the lake, Will told Amber all about his time with Tony. Will admired Amber for her interest and encouragement. Then as they neared their destination Will abruptly changed the subject.

"I have a few things I need to confess to you about the last time we were at the lake," he said.

"You mean way back in August at the campout?"

Will nodded. "I probably didn't show it, but I was pretty ticked about your being with Tony. I knew he was bad news for you, but I also knew you liked him. I wanted to trade places with him in the worst way."

"Will, you were jealous," Amber taunted playfully. Will blushed his admission of guilt.

"But there's something else," he continued. "Late that Saturday night I saw you sneak away from your tent. I wanted to try and talk some sense into you about Tony. So

I followed you in the shadows and saw you meet Tony in the woods."

"You watched what Tony did to me?" Amber gasped in shock.

"All I saw was a little drinking and kissing. Then I got so mad at him and so mad at you I went back to my tent. That's when I first told God to do something about Tony Ortiz."

Amber was quiet for several moments as if reliving the painful memories of her rebellion from God, which included her involvement with Tony. Will respected her silence until they drove into the parking area at the lake and stopped. He looked out across the lake and saw Tony skiing behind Duane's Bayliner.

"As long as I'm into true confessions," Will continued, averting Amber's eyes, "I have to tell you something else. I'm ashamed to admit that when the Commandos first started, I didn't want Tony to become a Christian. I thought for sure that if he trusted Christ the two of you would get together again, and you would be out of my life forever."

Amber said nothing. Will glanced at her, and he thought he read understanding and appreciation in her beautiful eyes.

"I have a true confession of my own, Will," she said at last, reaching out and taking his hand. "Last summer I was hung up on Tony Ortiz because he represented freedom from my parents. He was the key to the crowd I wanted to be with. But when I rediscovered God's unconditional love for me, that part of my life ended. I knew then that my next boyfriend would have to be someone who liked me for who I was, not for who I ran with. He would be somebody who enjoyed talking, joking, and having a good time without coming on like an octopus at the end of the evening. He would be someone who wanted to grow as a Christian as much as I do. And he would be cute."

Will could feel his temperature rising. Holding hands with Amber was bad enough, but to hear her talk like this made him feel out of breath, even though he'd been doing nothing but driving for two hours. It took every ounce of his strength just to maintain eye contact.

"For years you've been like a brother to me," Amber continued. "We've talked and laughed and had a great time. And since last summer we've been helping each other grow spiritually just like a brother and sister in Christ should. But last December when you held my hand at the Cunninghams' I suddenly realized that I didn't want you for a brother anymore." Will's eyes teared in emotion as he looked away. "Will, you're a sweet, caring, fun guy, and you're really cute too. You're the guy I want to be with."

Will's emotions suddenly seemed to go berserk inside him. He felt like laughing hysterically, crying for joy, and dancing like David before the Lord all in the same instant. Amber's warm hand touched his face, and Will looked deeply into her eyes. Slowly Amber leaned toward Will and kissed him tenderly on the cheek. As she moved back Will saw a tear trickle down her beautiful face.

"Let's commit our relationship to the Lord together," Will said softly. After a brief prayer, he added, "Now let's go water skiing!"

It wasn't a very warm day for water skiing, but everybody wanted at least one turn. The group had nearly doubled since summer, so two ski boats were in use. One of them was being driven by a guy from Duane's construction crew.

Will again got up on his first try. As he waved to Amber in the boat he flashed back to his first time on skis. Nine months earlier he looked like a bleached-out scarecrow bouncing across the water. Then he was about as tall as Amber and ten pounds lighter. Now he was closer to Tony Ortiz's height, and his scrawny frame had filled out about twenty pounds. He was still no Tony Ortiz on skis. But he got halfway around the lake this time before he crashed—and he didn't lose his swimsuit.

At sunset the group barbecued burgers around the same fire pit and sat eating them on the same logs as nine months earlier. The circle was jammed tight with bodies, but nobody seemed to mind. Will was especially happy that Amber was sitting on his side of the campfire. As Amber chatted with Hillary about the rally team's year-end party, Will munched on a burger and scanned the faces around him.

Tony Ortiz and Reggie Spencer were just a couple of weeks away from graduation. Reggie was discipling Tony now, and their friendship was stronger than ever. Tony's life had changed so drastically since Easter that three of his teammates had trusted Christ, including quarterback Tyrone Coleman. Tony and Ty had accepted scholarships to State University. They were even more excited about sharing their faith at State than about playing ball together.

Reggie, who had a job on Duane's construction crew after graduation, had been responsible for two members of the wild bunch trusting Christ, and they were both sitting with Reggie in the circle.

Will thought that Joy Akiyama had changed more than anyone in the last nine months. She was so open and talkative now. Her relationship with her parents was still very painful. But she was healing emotionally and her courageous spirit was contagious. One of her friends, a girl Joy was discipling, sat next to her.

As Will stared at Darcelle and Buster, he realized that their prayers had played a major role in what had happened to him since last summer. They were the original members of the youth group prayer team. Six kids had trusted Christ as a result of their witness this term, and two of them were in the circle with them.

Marlon Trask was missing from the circle. Will was still meeting with him once a week, but Marlon had decided to attend his uncle's church and try to encourage the youth group to join God's rescue operation. Two of his friends from the computer science class were with him. But Hillary

Putnam and the two girls she and Amber led to Christ were now full-fledged Liberation Commandos.

Jason Withers sat next to Marci Small, a girl he was dating from his drama class. Marci trusted Christ at the *Harvey* cast party. Will winced at how "normal" Jason seemed since meeting Marci. He hoped Jason would get over it.

"I think you all got to meet my friend, Mike Turcott," Duane said, interrupting Will's thoughts. "Mike and I work together, and he was kind enough to bring his boat up today so you could all ski. I've asked Mike to share something."

The Commandos gave Mike a cheer of thanks. He was a burly man in his mid-twenties, and he twirled a long stick in the fire as he spoke.

"I've had a pretty rough life," he said. "My parents kicked me out of the house when I was fifteen years old, and when I was eighteen I joined the Navy. I hung out with a bad crowd and learned to drink, gamble, and fight. I got so good at it that the Navy kicked me out.

"I bounced around from job to job, drinking and gambling away everything I earned. I finally got a job with Duane's construction crew. I settled down, got married, and started to live a decent life. Then last Christmas my wife left me for some other guy, and I went off the deep end again," Mike said with a slight choke in his voice.

"Duane has been talking to me about Christ ever since we started working together. So when I didn't show up for work for a couple of days, he came looking for me. He was like a real brother to me," he said smiling. "After a couple of weeks of helping me get my head straight, he shared the good news of God's unconditional love and forgiveness with me, and I trusted Christ as my Savior. Like a lot of you, my life has really changed. Knowing Christ personally is the greatest thing in the world."

The Commandos cheered again. Then Jason offered another one of the piercing insights for which he was becoming famous among his friends. "I've kind of been looking at the Commandos like a class in school. You sign up for it, you pass it, and then go on to something else. But after hearing Mike talk tonight, I think I've been looking at it all wrong. Being a Liberation Commando isn't something we stop doing during summer vacation or after we graduate. It's not like being in the real army where you serve for four years or eight years or twenty years and then get discharged.

"If Duane had stopped praying for people and sharing Christ when he left college, Mike might not have been saved," Jason added. "And if we think we can 'retire' next month or next year, there are all kinds of people in our lives who won't get saved. The devil won't give up until God finally burns him up. So the rescue mission must continue until Jesus comes back. We've been called to be liberators for life."

It was quiet for several moments except for the steady crackle of the campfire. Then Will spoke up. "I have a couple of things to say. First, this is Memorial Day, and I've really been enjoying the memories of what God has done in our group over the past nine months. But it may never have happened if it hadn't been for the teaching and encouragement and example of Duane and Liz." Will turned to the couple. "Thanks for letting God use you in our lives." The hills around Gilligan's Lake echoed with boisterous applause.

"Second, I agree with Jason. When we look around the circle and see the faces that weren't here last year—Tony, Hillary, Tyrone, Marci, and the rest, it's easy to feel like kicking back." Will continued, "But my father is still a captive in the darkness and so are some of your parents and brothers and sisters. Most of the kids at Ike High and State College are under Satan's control too. We still have a lot of praying and loving and sharing to do."

Will stood and walked over to the pile of lumber scraps Duane and Mike had brought along for firewood. He picked up a short section of two-by-four and held it up. "This represents me, and the campfire is God's mission to rescue the captives from the darkness." Then he tossed the wood into the fire. Sparks flew, and the flames hungrily surrounded the new log.

Jason was at Will's side immediately with his own hunk of wood. Amber, Tony, Duane, and Mike were right behind him. Will stepped aside as, one by one, his friends fed the flames with their logs of commitment. With every new log the campfire leaped higher. Soon the blaze lit up the campsite like daylight. Will wondered how large the fire would be by next Memorial Day.

The Prince of Darkness paced the Grand Chamber restlessly. The tyrannosaur had transformed himself into an oversized imitation of the Enemy's majestic lion. His discontented roars could be heard through the tunnels for several miles in every direction.

The lion had spent Memorial Day scourging an endless parade of his bumbling charges summoned from the divisions of his dark domain. Among them were Ratsbane, Stygios, and Nefarius, whose success at suppressing the uprising in Subsector 477 was questionable at best. Only a few captives had been liberated since the Easter-week ambush. But the rebels were growing in strength, and their prayers continued to shatter conduits and rock the cavern with the occasional appearances of sparkling brigadiers. Ratsbane barely escaped the Grand Chamber with his hide on this visit.

The lion paused to listen to the thundering waterfall of flames outside his chamber. The fire had ruled Satan's kingdom since the Enemy confined him there. And he knew that the Enemy's flames would eventually overrun the banks of the lake of fire and consume even him and his kingdom. "But not yet," the lion growled as he resumed his fitful pacing. "I will oppose the liberation of the captives with every mutant, runt, idea, and device at my command."

Suddenly the flames outside the Grand Chamber flickered brighter. A goon raced into the Chamber to report that the flare-up was caused by the rebels in Subsector 477 committing themselves to be liberators for life. Satan stepped to the archway and roared hatefully at the flames. He wondered how large the fire around him would be by next Memorial Day.

The Inside Story: Liberators for Life

When you stop to think about it, you'll probably only make a few lifetime commitments. As a Christian, you have committed yourself for life to be a disciple of Jesus Christ. And some day you'll probably say "I do," committing yourself to one marriage partner for life. But these days it's unlikely that you will stay in one career for life. Also, you probably won't live in the same house until you die. You may even live in different cities, states, or countries over the years. And you'll be lucky if you have one or two friends with whom you "go the distance."

But if you are serious about serving Christ from here on out, you need to understand one critical lifetime commitment that He has called you to make. Everyone Christ has rescued and called to be His disciple is also called to be a rescuer and a discipler of others. And just as He intends for you to be a disciple for life, He also calls you to be a discipler for life. Your commitment to pray for others, build bridges of love and concern to others, and share the gospel with others is a lifetime commitment.

COMMITTED "ALWAYS"

The lifetime nature of the call to be a liberator is written in God's Word. Just before He ascended to heaven, Jesus said to His disciples: "Go into all the world and preach the good news to all creation" (Mark 16:15). In Matthew 28:18–20, He made the command even clearer: "All authority in heaven and on earth has been given to me. Therefore go and make disciples of all nations, baptizing them in the name of the Father and of the Son and of the Holy Spirit, and teaching them to obey everything I have commanded you. And surely I am with you always, to the very end of the age."

These Scriptures describe what is called Christ's Great Commission. What does the Great Commission mean? It is the last and clearest—and one of the most important—commands Jesus gave His disciples. It means that everyone everywhere, whether on your campus or in another nation, should have the opportunity to say yes to Christ.

The Great Commission is a true expression of the heart of God (John 3:16). When the Great Commission is completed, Christ will return (Matthew 24:14).

Every Christian is to be involved in helping fulfill the Great Commission. Why? First, because it's a command, and the Scriptures say that if we love Christ we will obey His commands (John 14:23). Second, because there will always be people around you who need to hear the gospel and be discipled. As you are involved in helping fulfill the Great Commission, Christ promises to be with you always, because you need Him always in your lifetime ministry of reaching others.

Does this mean that God wants you to give up your dreams for a career so you can become a full-time evangelist, campus worker, pastor, or missionary? Not necessarily. What you do as a career is not the primary issue. The important thing is that you are seeking God's will for your life. And no matter what He calls you to do, you should plan on serving Him through your career to help fulfill the Great Commission.

What does it mean to be a lifetime Great Commission "commando"? It simply means:

- You always have a list of non-Christians for whom you are praying by name (family members, friends, classmates, neighbors, people you work with).

- You are always in the process of relating to and building bridges of communication with the non-Christians God is calling you to reach.

- You are always prepared to take the initiative and share a clear, simple presentation of the gospel with those around you who don't know Christ and persuade them to respond by trusting Christ.

- You are always ready to commit yourself to follow up and disciple those who trust Christ.

A LIFETIME LIFESTYLE

Being a lifetime liberator isn't a job; it's a lifestyle. So as one who is always to be ready to rescue non-Christians from the dominion of Satan, be aware that:

- You don't punch in at nine and punch out at five as a sharer of the good news. People under Satan's dominion are in chains twenty-four hours a day. So whether you're at school, at work, in a restaurant, at a game, at a party, or wherever, you're on duty as a liberator twenty-four hours a day.

- You don't get to retire. There's never going to be a time in your life when you can say, "Well, I've put in my thirty years. I'm done!" God has two ways to let you know when to stop: RIP or Rapture. Until then, you're still on active duty as a liberator.

If you're tempted to think that being a Liberation Commando is a chore, remember several things:

- You are privileged to join with God in His mission to liberate those in darkness. Think of what He's done for you. Consider what you have inherited as His child. Sharing Him with others as a lifetime liberator is a way to worship Him and thank Him for rescuing you.

- You are empowered for what you are called to do. God has not only commissioned you for your role, He has provided every resource you need to carry it out. Sure, you will expend your own time, energy, and substance in sharing the gospel with others. But you're never really running on your own power. The Holy Spirit within you makes you completely adequate for the task.

- You will prevail. Satan's power to hold your non-Christian friends in darkness is limited. God's power to set them free is unlimited. As you allow yourself to be led and empowered by the Holy Spirit, and as you pray, prepare, and share the gospel in the Spirit's power, you will see non-Christians rescued from the dominion of darkness and transferred into the kingdom of God.

FROM ADDITION TO MULTIPLICATION

You may be thinking, "Jesus told me to go into all the world and make disciples. But even if five of us won twenty-five people to Christ every day for the next twenty-five years, that would still only be a million people. That's kind of a drop in the bucket with more than 4 billion people in the world."

There are two ways to look at the ministry of a lifetime liberator. First, there is the strategy of spiritual addition. You share the gospel with unbelievers, they trust Christ, and the total increases with each new believer. If you were able to win a million people to Christ in your lifetime—or even a fraction of that—it would be great. But your efforts wouldn't come close to reaching the world.

The second strategy, which is the biblical strategy, is that of multiplication. Say that you and your four friends each won three people to Christ. Then in the course of a year you trained these fifteen people to be liberators also. In the second year, the five of you and your fifteen disciples each won and trained three more, and you continued the process year after year. In ten years there would be over half a million in your multiplication network. And in fifteen years you could reach the whole world!

Multiplying is God's strategy for populating the earth physically (Genesis 1:28) and for populating the kingdom of God spiritually. Paul instructed Timothy: "The things you have heard me say in the presence of many witnesses entrust to reliable men who will also be qualified to teach others" (2 Timothy 2:2). Paul discipled Timothy (among many others). Timothy discipled "reliable men" who, in turn, discipled "others."

God's plan is that you and your friends not only bring others to Christ, but that you equip those you win to be liberators of others. You may not trigger the ideal network that will reach the world's population with the gospel in fifteen years. But you will have the joy of knowing that you have participated in the rescue of hundreds, perhaps thousands, from Satan's kingdom. And that's really what it's all about.

Appendix

Would You Like to Know God Personally?

Yes, you can know God personally, as presumptuous as that may sound. God is so eager to establish a personal, loving relationship with you that He has already made all the arrangements. He is patiently and lovingly waiting for you to respond to His invitation. You can receive forgiveness of your sin and assurance of eternal life through faith in His only Son, the Lord Jesus Christ.

The major barrier that prevents us from knowing God personally is ignorance of who God is and what He has done for us. Read on and discover for yourself the joyful reality of knowing God personally.

The following four principles will help you discover how to know God personally and experience the abundant life He promised.

1. God loves you and created you to know Him personally.

(References should be read in context from the Bible wherever possible.)

God's Love

> For God so loved the world, that He gave His only begotten Son, that whoever believes in Him should not perish, but have eternal life.
>
> John 3:16

God's Plan

> Now, this is eternal life: that they may know you, the only true God, and Jesus Christ, whom you have sent.
>
> John 17:3

What prevents us from knowing God personally?

- Man is *sinful* and *separated* from God, so we cannot know Him personally or experience His love.

2. Man Is Sinful

> For all have sinned and fall short of the glory of God.
>
> Romans 3:23

Man was created to have fellowship with God; but, because of his stubborn self-will, he chose to go his own independent way, and fellowship with God was broken. This self-will, characterized by an attitude of active rebellion or passive indifference, is evidence of what the Bible calls sin.

Man Is Separated

> For the wages of sin is death [spiritual separation from God].
>
> Romans 6:23

This diagram illustrates that God is holy and man is sinful. A great gulf separates the two. The arrows illustrate that man is continually trying to reach God and establish a personal relationship with Him through his own efforts, such as a good life, philosophy, or religion.

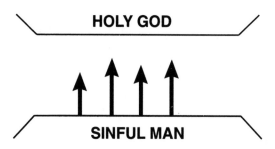

The third principle explains the only way to bridge this gulf . . .

- Jesus Christ is God's *only* provision for man's sin. Through Him alone we can know God personally and experience His love.

3. He Died in Our Place

But God demonstrates His own love toward us, in that while we were yet sinners, Christ died for us.

Romans 5:8

He Rose From the Dead

Christ died for our sins . . . He was buried . . . He was raised on the third day, according to the Scriptures . . . He appeared to Peter, then to the twelve. After that He appeared to more than five hundred.

1 Corinthians 15:3–6

He Is the Only Way to God

> Jesus said to him, "I am the way, and the truth, and the life; no one comes to the Father, but through me."
>
> John 14:6

This diagram illustrates that God has bridged the gulf which separates us from Him by sending His Son, Jesus Christ, to die on the cross in our place to pay the penalty for our sins.

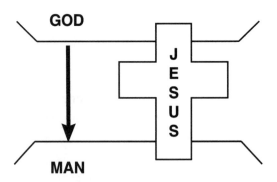

It is not enough to know these three laws, nor even to give intellectual assent to them . . .

It is not enough just to know these truths . . .

- We must individually *receive* Jesus Christ as savior and lord; then we can know God personally and experience His love.

4. We Must Receive Christ

But as many as received Him, to them He gave the right to become children of God, even to those who believe in His name.

John 1:12

We Receive Christ Through Faith

For by grace you have been saved through faith; and that not of yourselves, it is the gift of God; not as a result of works, that no one should boast.

Ephesians 2:8–9

When We Receive Christ, We Experience a New Birth

Read John 3:1–8.

We Receive Christ by Personal Invitation

[Jesus said:] Behold, I stand at the door and knock; if anyone hears My voice and opens the door, I will come in to Him.

Revelation 3:20

Receiving Christ involves turning to God from self (repentance) and trusting Christ to come into our lives to forgive our sins and to make us the kind of people He wants us to be. Just to agree intellectually that Jesus Christ is the Son of God and that He died on the cross for our sins is not enough. Nor is it enough to have an emotional experience. We receive Jesus Christ by faith, as an act of the will.

These two circles represent two kinds of lives:

SELF-DIRECTED LIFE
S —Self is on the throne
† ―-Christ is outside
      the life
● —Interests are directed
by self, often resulting in
discord and frustration

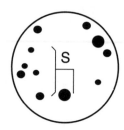

CHRIST-DIRECTED LIFE
† —Christ is in the life
      and on the throne
S —Self is yielding to Christ
● —Interests are directed
by Christ, resulting in
harmony with God's plan

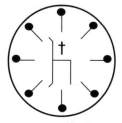

Which circle best represents your life?
Which circle would you like to have represent your life?
The following explains how you can invite Jesus Christ into your life.

You Can Receive Christ Right Now by Faith Through Prayer

Prayer is talking with God.

God knows your heart and is not so concerned with your words as He is with the attitude of your heart. The following is a suggested prayer:

Lord Jesus, I want to know You personally. Thank You for dying on the cross for my sins. I open the door of my life and receive You as my Savior and Lord. Thank You for forgiving my sins and giving me eternal life. Take control of the throne of my life. Make me the kind of person You want me to be.

Does this prayer express the desire of your heart?

If it does, pray this prayer right now, and Christ will come into your life, as He promised.

How to Know That Christ Is in Your Life

Did you receive Christ into your life? According to His promise in Revelation 3:20, where is Christ right now in relation to you? Christ said that He would come into your life and be your friend so you can know Him personally. Would He mislead you? On what authority do you know that God has answered your prayer? (The trustworthiness of God Himself and His Word.)

The Bible Promises Eternal Life to All Who Receive Christ

And the witness is this, that God has given us eternal life, and this life is in His Son. He who has the Son has the life; he who does not have the Son of God does not have the life. These things have I written to you who believe in the name of the Son of God, in order that you may know that you have eternal life.

1 John 5:11–13

Thank God often that Christ is in your life and that He will never leave you (Hebrews 13:5). You can know on the basis of His promise that Christ lives in you and that you have eternal life, from the very moment you invite Him in. He will not deceive you.

An important reminder...

Do Not Depend on Feelings

The promise of God's Word, the Bible—not our feelings—is our authority. The Christian lives by faith (trust) in the trustworthiness of God Himself and His Word. This train diagram illustrates the relationship between fact (God and His Word), faith (our trust in God and His Word), and feeling (the result of our faith and obedience) (John 14:21).

The train will run with or without the caboose. However, it would be useless to attempt to pull the train by the caboose. In the same way, we, as Christians, do not depend on feelings or emotions, but we place our faith (trust) in the trustworthiness of God and the promises of His Word.

Now That You Have Entered into a Personal Relationship with Christ

The moment that you received Christ by faith, as an act of the will, many things happened, including the following:

1. Christ came into your life (Revelation 3:20 and Colossians 1:27).

2. Your sins were forgiven (Colossians 1:14).

3. You became a child of God (John 1:12).

4. You received eternal life (John 5:24).

5. You began the great adventure for which God created you (John 10:10; 2 Corinthians 5:17; and 1 Thessalonians 5:18).

Can you think of anything more wonderful that could happen to you than entering into a personal relationship with Jesus Christ? Would you like to thank God in prayer right now for what He has done for you? By thanking God, you demonstrate your faith.

To enjoy your new relationship with God . . .

Suggestions for Christian Growth

Spiritual growth results from trusting Jesus Christ. "The righteous man shall live by faith" (Galatians 3:11). A life of faith will enable you to trust God increasingly with every detail of your life, and to practice the following:

G   Go to God in prayer daily (John 15:7).

R   Read God's Word daily (Acts 17:11)—begin with the Gospel of John.

O   Obey God moment by moment (John 14:21).

W   Witness for Christ by your life and words (Matthew 4:19; John 15:8).

T   Trust God for every detail of your life (1 Peter 5:7).

H   Holy Spirit—allow Him to control and empower your daily life and witness (Galatians 5:16–18; Acts 1:8).

Fellowship in a Good Church

God's Word admonishes us not to forsake "the assembling of ourselves together" (Hebrews 10:25). Several logs burn brightly together, but put one aside on the cold hearth and the fire goes out. So it is with your relationship with other Christians. If you do not belong to a church, do not wait to be invited. Take the initiative; call the pastor of a nearby church where Christ is honored and His Word is preached. Start this week, and make plans to attend regularly.

Additional Resources

BOOKS

The Teenage Q&A Book (Josh McDowell and Bill Jones)
Friend of the Lonely Heart (Josh McDowell and Norm Wakefield)
Don't Check Your Brains at the Door (Josh McDowell and Bob Hostetler)
Sex, Guilt, and Forgiveness (Josh McDowell)
It Can Happen to You—A Book on Date Rape (Josh McDowell)
Love, Dad (Josh McDowell)
Love, Sex, and Dating (book trilogy) (Bill Jones and Barry St. Clair)

VIDEO

The Teenage Q&A Video Series
Don't Check Your Brains at the Door Video Series
WHY WAIT? Video Collection:
    Why Waiting Is Worth the Wait
    God Is No Cosmic Kill-joy
    How to Handle the Pressure Lines
    A Clean Heart for a New Start
Let's Talk about Love and Sex
"No!"—The Positive Answer Video Series
Friend of the Lonely Heart Video Series
Who Do You Listen To? Music Video

AUDIO

Friend of the Lonely Heart (Josh McDowell and Norm Wakefield)
The Teenage Q&A Book on Tape
Why Wait? What You Need to Know about the Teen Sexuality
    Crisis (Josh McDowell and Dick Day)
The Secret of Loving
Why Waiting Is Worth the Wait

STUDY COURSES

So You Want to Get into the Race (Chuck Klein)
So You Want to Set the Pace (Chuck Klein)
So You Want Solutions (Chuck Klein)
How to Begin Group Outreach Events (Sonlife Ministries)
Evangelism Workbook (Sonlife Ministries)

Available from your Christian bookstore or from Word Publishing

---

GOING TO COLLEGE?

Some New Christian Friends
Are Already Waiting to Meet You!!

To connect with Christians and campus ministries at your college, contact Student LINC toll free at 1-800-678-LINC [5462].

Student LINC provides a centralized database where Campus Crusade for Christ, InterVarsity Christian Fellowship, and the Navigators have pooled their information about the locations of their ministries on campuses across the United States.

Student LINC can give you the name and phone number of the leader for each group on each campus. Also, if no strong Christian group is active on your campus, Student LINC can help you start one. For more information, just give them a call at 1-800-678-LINC [5462].

Don't leave home before calling!

ABOUT THE AUTHORS

JOSH McDOWELL is an internationally known speaker, author, and traveling representative of Campus Crusade for Christ. A graduate of Wheaton College and Talbot Theological Seminary, he has written more than thirty-five books and appeared in numerous films, videos, and television series. He and his wife Dottie live in Julian, California, with their four children.

CHUCK KLEIN is a well-traveled speaker and the national director of Student Venture, the high school outreach ministry of Campus Crusade for Christ and also the national director of the Community Group of Ministries for the U.S. Field of Campus Crusade. His publications include numerous student study courses, including the So You Want . . . series. He lives in San Diego, California, with his wife Clare and their three daughters.

ED STEWART is a former youth pastor and curriculum editor turned freelance writer. He has authored eight books himself and freelance written or edited more than forty books with other Christian authors. He and his wife Carol are the parents of two grown children and live in Hillsboro, Oregon.

LET'S STAY IN TOUCH

If you have grown personally as a result of this material, we should stay in touch. You will want to continue in your Christian growth, and to help your faith become even stronger, our team is constantly developing new materials.

We publish a monthly newsletter called **5 Minutes with Josh** which will (1) tell you about those new materials as they become available, (2) answer your tough questions, (3) give creative tips on being an effective parent, (4) let you know our ministry needs, and (5) keep you up to date on Josh McDowell's speaking schedule (so you can pray).

If you would like to receive this publication, send your name and address to Josh McDowell—**5 Minutes with Josh**, Campus Crusade for Christ, 100 Sunport Lane, Orlando, Fla. 32809.

OPERATION POWERLINK

PowerLink is a national evangelistic outreach campaign for youth groups across the nation. Youth groups will be participating in a video series outreach training course in preparation for inviting their non-Christian friends to their own locally sponsored "See You At the Party" event on March 6, 1993. The vision is that some fifty thousand youth groups across the nation will simultaneously conduct their own "See You At the Party"outreach by viewing a live-by-satellite broadcast featuring contemporary Christian music and a message by Josh McDowell.

In addition to *Under Siege*, you will also want to look for the *PowerLink Video Series*, a package of two videos (containing six sessions) featuring contemporary Christian music and testimonies by Josh McDowell and others. The video package includes a copy of *Under Siege, The PowerLink Youth Bible*, and a leader's guide.

The PowerLink Youth Bible is translated for today's teen and is based on the acclaimed, easy-to-read New Century Version. Added sidelights and real-life stories make this a powerful Bible that speaks to youth.